A Traveller's Guide to
ROYAL ROADS

Charles Kightly & Michael Cyprien

HTI

Historical Times INC.
Harrisburg

CONTENTS

Introduction 5

Boudicca TASBURGH-MANCETTER A.D. 60 Anne Ross
14

Alfred the Great CHIPPENHAM-WEDMORE 878 Anne Ross
28

William the Conqueror PEVENSEY-WESTMINSTER 1066 Trevor Rowley
43

William Rufus GLOUCESTER-WINCHESTER 1100 Anne Ross
58

King Stephen WAREHAM-OXFORD 1142 Anthony Goodman
70

King John KING'S LYNN-NEWARK 1216 John Steane
84

Edward I WORCESTER-CONWY 1282/3 John Steane
98

Eleanor of Castile HARBY-WESTMINSTER 1290 John Steane
113

Further reading 128

First published in 1985 by Historical Times Incorporated,
2245 Kohn Road, Harrisburg, PA 17105, USA
and by Routledge & Kegan Paul plc
14 Leicester Square, London WC2H 7PH, England
9 Park Street, Boston, Mass. 02108, USA
464 St Kilda Road, Melbourne, Victoria 3004, Australia, and
Broadway House, Newton Road, Henley on Thames, Oxon RG9 1EN, England

Photography and Art Direction by Michael Cyprien

Printed in England by BAS Printers Limited,
Over Wallop, Stockbridge, Hampshire

ISBN 0 918678 09 9

INTRODUCTION

Even now, the monarch of Britain leads a far from sedentary life. For though her usual home is Buckingham Palace in London, she is very often to be found instead in the royal apartments at Windsor Castle, or at such official residences as Holyrood House in Edinburgh: part of each year, too, is spent at her holiday retreats at Sandringham in Norfolk and Balmoral in Aberdeenshire, and scarcely a month passes without a demanding round of state visits. Yet compared with their royal ancestors of the Anglo-Saxon and medieval periods, twentieth-century sovereigns are sluggish stay-at-homes, whose existence is a model of order, quietness and stability. For the rulers included in this book travelled incessantly, and many spent almost the whole of their reigns continually moving from place to place, endlessly "gyrating" from palace to monastery and from castle to hunting-lodge along the royal roads of Britain.

The much-maligned King John, for example, shifted his residence an average of twelve times a month throughout his reign: and even his twenty or so most favoured "homes" rarely held him for more than two or three days at a time. While his father Henry II spent the thirty-four Christmasses of his reign in twenty-four different places, ranging from Nottingham to Bordeaux in southern France, and from Dublin to Bayeux in Normandy. Henry and John, admittedly, were members of the Angevin family: whose diabolical energy (like Henry's fits of violent rage, when he rolled on the floor and gnawed rushes) was supposedly inherited from the she-devil among their ancestors. But their habit of incessant travelling was by no means exceptional, either among their medieval fellow-sovereigns or the other notable men and women of their day.

What was it that impelled these rulers to spend so much time – as Henry II's courtier-poet Walter Map put it – "wandering eternally without stop or stay"? Not whim or comfort, assuredly, for life on the roads of medieval Britain was scarcely a holiday: and it is surely no accident that both Alfred and Stephen suffered from the painful and humiliating affliction of piles, probably caused by much hard riding; while John, Eleanor and Edward I were all to die of diseases which were at least exacerbated by their ceaseless travels.

To the earlier Anglo-Saxon kings, however, such continual journeyings were a necessity of life. For, living as they did at a period when the idea of a money-economy was only just developing, they collected their rents instead in the form of food and drink. Such provisions could, of course, be despatched to the place where the king happened to be in residence: but given the difficulties of transport and also the total lack of means for preserving food, they might very well be inedible by the time they reached him. So it was clearly more practical for the King to travel to the provisions, and literally to eat his way round his dominions at his subjects' expense.

By Alfred's time, kings had ceased to live entirely off the land in this manner, and many of the old "food-rents" had been transformed into cash payments: but he and his Anglo-Saxon descendants could still expect free entertainment from the noblemen they visited on their travels, and even after the Norman Conquest William Rufus seems to have collected rents in hospitality and hunting arrows during his last fateful journey through the New Forest. Not until the reign of Rufus's successor Henry I, indeed, were food-rents finally abolished: and by then the habit of continual journeying they had engendered had become habitual to the English monarchy.

The incessant gyrations of early medieval sovereigns, however, were far from being merely a matter of tradition. For, in the absence of any form of mass communication, kings must be seen – and seen to rule – by as many of their subjects as possible. As an act of deliberate policy, therefore, the Norman kings held ceremonial "crownwearings" at each of the great festivals of the church: generally appearing at Easter in the old Saxon capital of Winchester; at Whitsun in Westminster; and at Christmas in Gloucester. There – or wherever more pressing needs found them at the appropriate season – they displayed themselves in full state, seated on a throne and decked in all the robes and regalia of power.

But early medieval kings were not simply distant and almost-divine rulers, as their successors were later to become. They were also, quite literally, the government: and wherever the king happened to be – in York or Guildford, a hunting lodge in the New Forest or a small village in Norfolk – was the capital of England, if only for a few days. The monarch's journeyings, therefore, were to a very great extent the means by which all government was carried on; and with him travelled not only his own royal household, but also the great departments of state. During much of the period covered by this book, indeed, household and government departments were virtually indistinguishable. By the twelfth century, admittedly, some of the financial officials of the Exchequer had taken up permanent residence at Winchester or London, abandoning with a sigh of relief the appalling responsibility of trailing after the king with hundreds of barrels of silver pennies – which were the only coin then minted. But much of the civil service continued permanently on the road throughout our period: and from its ever temporary quarters in castle or tent issued a stream of writs, dealing with every aspect of administration from the grant of a confiscated manor to the payment for transporting Queen Eleanor's favourite chestnuts. Addressed daily from wherever the king chose to lay his head, and interrupted only at times of crisis or royal bereavement, such records enable us to trace the routes of the endless court progresses.

A travelling capital and an itinerant household, the royal retinue was also a mobile court of justice. So famous was Henry II's justice – at least according to Walter Map – that anyone with a good case would pursue the royal court on its progress, in the hope of appearing before him. Those with a bad conscience, conversely, had to be dragged after him by force: and so too – in closely guarded carts – did the accusers and accused in certain criminal cases, who must fight judicial duels in the kings presence. God, it was believed, would infallibly then intervene on the side of right: and the unsuccessful combatant, if not fatally wounded in the duel, would be strung up forthwith from the nearest tree.

In time of war – which is to say virtually the whole of Stephen's reign, much of Alfred's and Edward I's, and the climax of John's – the travelling court frequently became the nucleus and headquarters of a great marching army, led by the king against rebellious barons, rival claimants to the throne, or foreign foes. While in happier times (or indeed whenever the opportunity arose) the progress took on the holiday atmosphere of a vast hunting expedition, with the added bonus of fresh venison and game for the court at the end of the day. But it was the sport that counted: for Alfred, William the Conqueror, William Rufus and John were all alike passionately addicted to hunting. The Conqueror it was, indeed, who began the process by which almost a quarter of the land-area of England became "royal forests", the personal hunting preserves of the monarch.

There were, then, a number of reasons why medieval kings spent so much of their lives travelling the royal roads of Britain. As landowners, they had originally needed to live off the produce of their personal estates; and in later centuries they found it equally necessary to oversee the efficient running of their manors – a visit from the king himself being worth any number of letters to stewards. As monarchs, they needed to be seen by their subjects, to govern their realm in person, and to dispense justice far and wide. As war-leaders, they must defend their territories and harry those of their enemies: and as men they loved to hunt their great private forests. Many royal progresses, indeed, combined most if not all of these functions: and in order to do so, kings inevitably travelled with a lengthy train of retainers, advisers, clerks and servants.

At the heart of the whole itinerant court, of course, was the monarch himself, accompanied by his intimate friends and surrounded by his personal bodyguard – Alfred's oath-bound Saxon "companions", a troop of John's hated but faithful and efficient mercenaries, or Edward I's customary twenty-four archers. Not far from the king, too, would be senior members of the royal household-cum-travelling civil service, whose Latin name of *familia* well expresses its essential nature. For the household was indeed a kind of "family": whose members, continually in the monarch's eye as they were, stood a more than equal chance of snapping up any well-paid appointments which might fall vacant. Even the lesser members of the household-family (like Queen Eleanor's coachman Christian Page) could hope for a pension when they grew infirm: and for all there was the attraction of free clothing, or "livery", and a daily allowance of food, drink and candles.

According to a document drawn up at the beginning of Stephen's reign, these allowances ranged from the chancellor's princely five shillings a day, with a loaf of "lord's" or "simnel" bread, two salted simnels, one measure of "clear" and one of "ordinary" wine, with one great wax candle and forty candle-ends; down to the night-watchmens' daily penny-halfpenny, with four candles, two rough loaves, and a gallon of beer – which was, understandably, issued only after they had done their night's work. The chancellor, as the king's chief minister and head of the civil service, was the leading member of the household: but only just below him in status were the heads of department, namely the steward (who oversaw the hall, kitchen, and larder); the butler (who had the important responsibility of keeping king and court supplied with wine); the treasurer; and the chamberlain. This last official was closest to the king of all, for he it was who presided over the monarch's travelling bed-chamber and took care that all his most personal needs were catered for. In King John's day, therefore, the equipment in his charge included the sovereign's portable urinal and his bathtub: and his staff included an "usher" to make the king's bed, Florence the royal washerwoman, Ralph the king's tailor and William the bathman. For, with all his faults, John was scrupulously clean by the standard of his time, and fond of his comfort: he was, for example, the first English king known to have possessed a dressing-gown, and the first recorded royal user of sugar.

Then there were the "outdoor" officials, the constable and the marshals. The first had particular responsibility for the horses and carriages so vital to the travelling household: and also for the multifarious grooms and huntsmen – falconers, kennelmen, wolf-hunters and even wildcat-hunters – who ministered to the king's favourite sport. The marshals included among their tasks the maintenance of law and order in and around the itinerant court. Under their jurisdiction fell not only all known criminals arrested within twelve leagues of the place where the king lay: but also the crowd of suitors and the rag-tag of unofficial and generally disreputable hangers-on who invariably followed a royal progress. Harlots, apparently, were a particular problem – though not always to Henry II, who fathered on "a common woman called Ykenai" a child who grew up to be Archbishop of York: and under Edward I the marshals were empowered to fine these fourpence for a first offence, to shave off their hair for a third and, for a fourth, to cut off their upper lip "so that none should afterwards desire them".

Not least among the household servants, moreover, were the "sumptermen" responsible for packing and transporting every item used by the court, and the scores of tents which were erected to house its various departments. Everything, therefore, had to be capable of being folded into a saddle-bag, or stowed into a "sumpter" chest for carriage on a pack-horse or in a two-wheeled cart. More valuable or fragile articles, like the king's "wardrobe" of rich clothes, jewels and personal possessions, might warrant a special four-wheeled waggon: while the ladies of the court – especially if they were pregnant or infirm, or if the weather was bad—travelled either in swaying "litters" slung between two horses, or in more comfortable and elaborate carriages.

Most members of the itinerant court preferred to ride rather than travel in carriages. Kings and knights, in time of war or when ceremonially entering a town or castle, might temporarily mount a fierce and showy "great horse" or *destrier*: but on the open road (if they had any sense) they would quickly exchange this for a more comfortable and less belligerent riding horse, probably a well-bred but quiet *palfrey* or, for the more corpulent, a strong *rouncy*. Ladies (who in early medieval times rode astride rather than side-saddle) favoured a small and dainty *jennet*; and richer clerks affected an expensive smooth-paced mule: while lesser folk made do with a *hackney* or a spare pack-horse, and proletarian hangers-on rode anything more or less horse-shaped they could find.

Even the most dubious of riding horses, however, could move much faster than the lumbering vehicles of the baggage-train: and it is clear that the king's mounted party would frequent separate itself from the baggage, diverting from the main road for a day or two's hunting while the waggons creaked by a more direct route to some ordained rendezvous. On the most famous of such occasions, John's baggage-train was engulfed by the sands of the Wash. But lesser disasters could well occur if the king suddenly changed his mind about his destination after the baggage had set off, so that the banquetting plate arrived at Winchester at about the same time as the sovereign wanted his dinner at Clarendon. On occasion, therefore, life in the mobile village that was the royal court could be anything but a picnic: and Walter Map complained vividly "we travel with carts and pack-horses, pack-saddles and panniers, falcons and dogs, and a great crowd of men and women . . . we lay waste whole kingdoms, wear out our clothes, our bodies and our horses . . . in vain and entirely unfruitful haste we are borne on our insane course". In fact, he concluded, "the court is truly a place of punishment, and only in this one respect is it less dreadful than Hell, in that those whom the court torments can at least escape by dying."

It was all very well for the witty Map to joke in this way. But for the unfortunate inhabitants of the areas through which the royal progress journeyed, its passage could be anything but a laughing matter. The approach of William Rufus's notoriously unruly travelling court, for example, so terrified countrymen that they fled for refuge to the woods and hills: and though a clause in Magna Carta specifically prohibited the king's ministers from arbitrarily commandeering horses or carts from the villages they passed through, medieval village bailiffs were continually either protesting that waggons had been taken at harvest-time and never returned, or bribing officials to look elsewhere for their transport.

What kind of roads did royal progresses travel, on their endless journeyings about the land? The basis of early medieval long-distance communications was the network of Roman roads built between A.D. 43 and A.D. 410; whose marvellously direct alignments, indeed, still stand out clearly on modern road maps. For their routes were so well chosen that many continue in use today: a fact startlingly apparent to the car-borne traveller approaching Cirencester – a principal hub of the Roman system – along any one of the dead-straight modernised Roman roads which still converge on it from almost every point of the compass.

The greatest of these Roman roads originated as the routes of the conquering Roman armies, who never advanced without establishing a direct and defended line of communication to their base. Along this rudimentary but carefully guarded track, supplies and reinforcements could safely travel up to the front: and down it, should this become necessary, the legions could either retire or – as occurred in the war against Boudicca – counter-march to deal with an enemy in their rear. The campaign successfully completed, the rough supply line became a properly surveyed and engineered road, with a "metalled" or stone-paved surface, often raised on an embankment and generally flanked by side-ditches for drainage. When kept in good repair, such roads allowed travel at a speed unprecedented in the ancient world: and Boudicca, turning her enemy's weapon against him, made full use of them during her bloody and revengeful struggle for liberation.

In all, the Romans built between eight and ten thousand miles of roads during their occupation of Britain: though not all of these were entirely new "campaign roads", for some, like the Foss Way from Exeter to Lincoln, the Icknield Way from Salisbury Plain to the Wash, or the post-Boudiccan road from Colchester to Caistor-by-Norwich – approximately followed the line of already-ancient prehistoric trackways. Roman Britain, therefore, possessed a highly efficient communications system: but during the centuries of obscure anarchy which followed the collapse of Roman government in A.D. 410, the great majority at least of minor roads appear to have fallen into partial or total disrepair and disuse.

Yet longer-distance trackways also existed, being frequently called *haerepaths* or *harroways*, from the Anglo-Saxon words meaning "army roads": and it was along one of these (still named "the Hardway"., but now a minor road linking the B3081 at Redlynch to the B3092 near Stourton, Wiltshire) that Alfred and his men must have ridden to the trysting place before their great victory at Edington. That the major Roman arterial roads continued in some kind of use throughout the Saxon period, moreover, is evidenced by the fact that their present names are invariably of Anglo-Saxon origin: thus the legionary road from Exeter to Lincoln became "the Foss Way" from its Roman "fosses" or side-ditches; while the route from Dover via London to Chester became "Watling Street", "the way to St Albans", which the Saxons called *Waetlingacaestir.*

There is no doubt, at any rate, that these arterial routes were thronged with traffic during the early middle ages: and every one of the medieval royal progresses described in this book travelled to some extent along Roman roads. By the twelfth century, indeed, the "four great roads of England" – The Foss Way, the Icknield Way, Watling Street and Ermine Street, which ran from London to Lincoln and York – had been officially classified as *chimini regales*, or "royal roads". As such, they were under the king's direct protection, and any crime or assault committed on or near them was punishable by particularly heavy penalties: contemporary records also suggest that they were paved with stone, and kept in repair, while each of them was required by law to be wide enough to allow two waggons to pass, or for sixteen armoured knights to ride along them abreast.

These, then, were special cases: but all major medieval roads – many of which had no Roman ancestry – were regarded as "the king's highway", and it was clearly in the interests of the eternally travelling monarchs to keep them in as good and safe a condition as possible. Thus, in 1285, Edward I required a distance of 200 feet on either side of all roads to be cleared of under-growth, in order to foil the "sackpurses and roberdesmen" who were "accustomed to crouch in hedges and ditches by the highway, lying in wait to beat, maim, rob and slay the people".

There was, however, little centralised planning of new routes in the medieval period – Edward's campaign roads into Wales were exceptional – and the upkeep of the English communications system was left either to the somewhat desultory attention of local landowners or to the generosity of pious benefactors. Many, indeed, hoped to save their souls by the "amending of evil ways and feeble bridges" or the reconstruction of "perilous and muddy causeways". All this – together with numerous contemporary records of pack-horses disappearing into bogs, royal messengers "drowned and devoured by wild beasts" after falling from a ricketty bridge, and passers-by (even in Westminster) "suddenly falling into a pit in the way, so that many bones of their bodies were broken" – gives the impression that medieval roads were extremely hazardous, and certainly their condition was appalling by modern standards.

Yet it must be remembered that the evidence against medieval roads (which are usually mentioned only when they were bad) is to some extent balanced by the silence of satisfied travellers. Chaucer, for example, scarcely mentions the condition of the roads along which his Canterbury Pilgrims rode: while John Leland, who at the end of the middle ages traversed thousands of miles of English highways, complains of them only very occasionally. Nor, if the roads of the thirteenth century were as ill-made as some maintain, could King John's itinerant court ever have managed its frequent journeys of thirty-five, forty, or even fifty miles a day.

The modern car-borne traveller, of course, will have no difficulty keeping up with John's breakneck dashes, or indeed in following the footsteps of any of the royal progresses described. For the medieval road system is still substantially intact and in use, even though many once-busy medieval highways have now declined into quiet back lanes or, conversely, developed into modern dual carriageways, by-passing most of the towns and villages through which the royal travellers journeyed.

Here a word of warning is perhaps necessary. Modern travellers, however closely they follow the route of Alfred or William Rufus, will naturally pass through a landscape which has changed considerably since the early medieval period: and even where the modern road covers precisely the same ground as its medieval predecessor – as, for example, parts of the present A2 from Dover to Canterbury follow almost exactly the Conqueror's line of march – the road itself will have altered its appearance. To be passable at all by modern traffic, in fact, the royal highways of medieval Britain must necessarily have become modern roads, and in this process much of their original character has inevitably been lost. Only where medieval roads have been ignored by progress, therefore, is it possible to see them as our royal travellers saw them: and in such cases they can be traversed only by leaving the car and exploring on foot. To the west of Malmesbury in Wiltshire, for instance, the unimproved Foss Way still exists in the form of a series of muddy tracks and greenways, marching in an absolutely straight line across the countryside. This is accessible either where it crosses the B4040 from Malmesbury to Easton Grey (at OS 173 SU 893877) or from the B4014 from Malmesbury to Tetbury (at OS 173 SU 915909): and a short walk from either of these points will show us the road much as it was used by Stephen in 1142, and by countless other medieval travellers.

But if the landscapes and roads of medieval Britain have changed somewhat, a very great deal remains as it was when our royal progresses passed by. With the aid of this book, the modern traveller too can enjoy the castles, monasteries, churches and villages so closely associated with his kingly predecessors on their journeys about the land: and at the same time gain a rich and unique insight into the history of the nation. Accompanying these rewarding modern itineraries will be four expert guides.

Anthony Goodman (who describes Stephen's journey) read History at Magdalen College, Oxford, and is now Reader in History at the University of Edinburgh. He is particularly interested in English medieval history, and is well known as the author of *The Loyal Conspiracy* (Routledge 1971); *A History of England from Edward II to James I* (Longman 1977); and *The Wars of the Roses* (Routledge 1981).

Dr Anne Ross (who writes about Boudicca, Alfred and William Rufus) obtained her Doctorate in Celtic Studies, Archaeology and History at the University of Edinburgh. Dr Ross, a Gaelic speaker, has collected oral traditions in Scotland: and has written, lectured and broadcast widely on Celtic language and literature, and especially the interaction of Celts with Romans, Saxons, Scandinavians and Normans down the centuries. Her best-known book is *Pagan Celtic Britain* (Routledge 1967).

Trevor Rowley, MA, M.Litt., FSA, MIFA (who writes about William the Conqueror) is a Geography graduate of University College, London; and is at present Staff Tutor in Archaeology and Local Studies at the Oxford University Department for External Studies. Among his many publications are *Villages in the Landscape* (Dent 1978); *The Norman Heritage* (Routledge 1983); and *The High Middle Ages* (Routledge 1985).

John Steane, MA, FSA (who describes the journeys of John, Edward I and Eleanor) read Modern History at Magdalen College, Oxford. Keeper of the Field Section at the Oxfordshire County Museum, he is the author of numerous papers and books on medieval archaeology and landscape history, including *The Northamptonshire Landscape* (Hodder and Stoughton 1974) and *The Archaeology of Medieval England and Wales* (1984).

The excellent Ordnance Survey Landranger maps will prove invaluable in locating the sites. These maps are widely available; their reference numbers and National Grid coordinates accompany each site entry.

Charles Kightly, York 1985

Boudicca
The trail of the Queen's revenge
TASBURGH–MANCETTER A.D. 60

Anne Ross

When the Romans started the conquest of Britain in A.D. 43, the king of the Iceni, a tribe living in what was later to be called East Anglia, submitted and continued to rule as a Roman client. When King Prasutagus of the Iceni died in 59, leaving a widow, Boudicca, and two young daughters, the Romans considered the Emperor Nero to be his heir. Their attempted takeover provoked opposition. Boudicca led the tribe in revolt, allied with their southern neighbours, the Trinovantes. The Britons destroyed the colony of Roman army veterans at Colchester (*Camulodunum*), whose inhabitants vainly sought refuge in the imposing temple there, dedicated to the *numen* (divine spirit) of the emperor. Roman relief forces were too weak to protect London and St Albans (*Verulamium*) from British atrocities and destruction. But Boudicca's forces were soon afterwards overwhelmed by the army scrambled together by the governor Suetonius Paulinus. She then died, either by taking poison, or of disease. Her place of burial is unknown. The Iceni endured Roman revenge and full incorporation into the province.

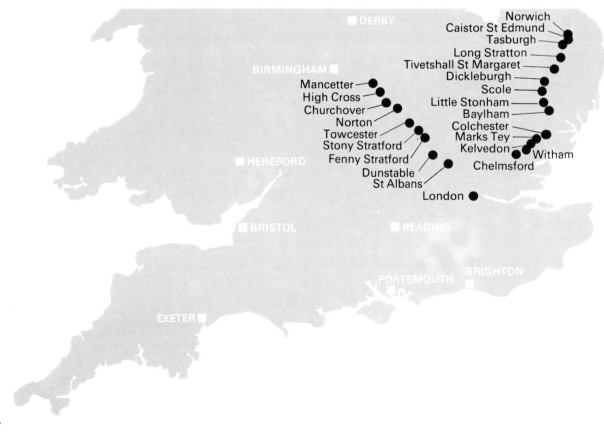

"She was huge of frame, terrifying of aspect, and with a harsh voice. A great mass of bright red hair fell to her knees: she wore a twisted golden necklace, and a tunic of many colours, over which was a thick mantle, fastened by a brooch. Now she grasped a spear, to strike fear into all who watched her . . ." Thus wrote the Roman historian Dio Cassius.

The name Boudicca (Boadicea, Boadicia, Bonduca, as it came variously to be spelled) means "Victory" or "Victoria" (Welsh, *buddug*). Her story, insofar as we have knowledge of it, has been the subject of many accounts by scholars, one of the most imaginative being by Dudley and Webster (1962) whose work is listed in the bibliography. The traveller will find here discussion and detail of the action and progress summarised below.

Born about A.D. 20 in the royal household of the powerful Celtic tribe, the Iceni of what is now Norfolk, she grew up in turbulent and distressing times. For the tribal system still prevailed among the British; and although there could be temporary amalgams of tribes, the centres of power tended to drift, with consequent strife and disorganisation, which rendered them easy prey to Roman commanders.

After the successful invasion under Claudius (A.D. 43), eleven British kings are said to have surrendered to the Romans, either peaceably or after defeat. The Icenian king accepted the Romans without a fight. We can see how such an arrangement would appear attractive to the Iceni, who had apparently enjoyed good diplomatic relations with the Romans even before the invasion, and regarded them as an ally against their aggressive British neighbours the Catuvellauni. Their ruler went in good faith to Colchester to receive the privileged status of client-king, and a degree of independence accorded to only one other British tribe. Thus, however, he unwittingly sowed the seeds of the events of seventeen years afterwards.

Until the death of Prasutagus – Boudicca's husband, who became King of the Iceni in about A.D. 48 – in A.D. 59, things were tranquil and prosperous with the Iceni, although troubles of various kinds were beginning to fester. In the year 57 a policy of increasing taxes was put into force, in an attempt by the Romans to recover some of the expenses of the military campaigns – or to pay off the Emperor Nero's creditors. Suetonius now succeeded as Governor of Britain.

The royal seat of the reputedly wealthy Icenian ruling family seems likely to have been at Tasburgh, eight miles south of Norwich. Prasutagus married Boudicca in about A.D. 43, and we know they had two daughters. When Prasutagus died, Boudicca naturally succeeded as queen, according to accepted custom in the Celtic world, where a powerful queen, warrior and priestess, was in no way exceptional.

In his will, Prasutagus made the Emperor co-heir with his daughters, "in the belief that this mark of attention would result in the kingdom and his household escaping harm". There was, however, no suggestion that the client kingship should be perpetuated. Prasutagus had the future of his people at heart; but in spite of his efforts to secure their well-being, the Iceni were to meet with uncivilised brutality after the death of their king.

It seems that certain monies given by Claudius to the British kings were now to be looked on, not as gifts, but as repayable loans, with accumulated interest – a crippling visitation on taxpayers. Prasutagus may have thought

Agricultural land that was once within the defensive ramparts of Tasburgh's extensive hillfort

that his legacy to Rome would cover all his obligations in that quarter; but the Procurator or chief Roman financial agent in Britain (one Catus Decianus) thought otherwise, and acted as if the whole territory had been made over to Rome. The estates of the kinsmen of the royal household were seized, and aristocrats and commoners alike sold into slavery. With true Roman thoroughness the king's widow, Boudicca, was flogged, and her daughters savagely raped. Such conduct fanned the already-flickering flames of unrest, and put the burning brand into the hand of the outraged Icenian queen.

The Roman military commander Suetonius was occupied with his campaign in north Wales, to the exclusion of what was happening in his distant rear. Meanwhile, in the east the Britons held conferences at which "they compared their grievances, and inflamed each other by the constructions they put on them". We do not know how many tribes took part during this period of preparation. The Iceni and the Essex Trinovantes were at the core of resistance: and the Hertfordshire Catuvellauni, the Coritani of modern Leicestershire, the Shropshire Cornovii, the Gloucestershire Dobunni, the Durotriges of Dorset and the far-off Brigantes of the north all may have contributed and played a part. One report asserts that 120,000 men were hosted; and even if this may err considerably on the large side, it is indicative of the numbers of Britons involved in the great attempt. Dedicated to religious observance, they believed their gods were on their side. They had complete faith in their courageous queen.

Her valour, and the extraordinary support she received from the truculent tribesmen of the island, made her rebellion a threat, not only to the Empire in Britain, but also to the Empire in Europe. Had she won the day against Suetonius Paulinus, the course of British and European history might have been quite altered. Celtic might have become the dominant language. Celtic laws and religion and the old Celtic culture might have continued – the ancient culture, enriched by contact with Rome, might have blossomed. Her defeat earned for her the laurels of a victor; her name is still legend among those who venerate true heroism – victory in defeat. For, according to the Romans, the British queen perished by her own hand, by means of poison.

This, then, is the course of the progress of Boudicca, queen of the Iceni, at the head of the army of Britain bent on freeing their country from the invader.

In the year A.D. 60, the low-lying hillfort at **Tasburgh**, eight miles south of the city of **Norwich** (which did not then exist) was the largest of such in the territory of the Iceni. In the absence of any proof to the contrary, it may be assumed that this was the headquarters of the Icenian tribe in the years prior to the Boudiccan campaign. Support is given to this proposition, moreover, by the fact that when a new, romanised tribal capital was established ten years later, it was sited five miles north of Tasburgh, at **Caistor St Edmund**, and given the name *Venta Icenorum*. For there are other examples of the Roman authorities selecting a new site for a tribal capital near, rather than at, an old one. At Colchester, for example, there was a gap of some two miles between the old and the new towns; at Maiden

TASBURGH Norfolk
TM 201960 OS 134
Tasburgh is seven miles south of Norwich, half a mile along a secondary road leading west off the A140.

The low-lying hillfort occupying the promontory rising above the east bank of the River Tas measured some twenty-four acres in extent, within a stout rampart and ditch. All that now remains of these are stretches of shallow scarps, or slopes, in the fields on either side of the road leading north out of the village from the road-junction east of the church. The earliest reference to the place is in the Domesday Book (1086), where the name appears as "Taseburc" – which accounts for the modern pronunciation Tazeburgh, not Tassburgh. This is a purely Anglo-Saxon word, reflecting nothing of the prehistoric or Romano-British name of the place.

When the traveller immersed in the ethos of Tasburgh looks round, the most striking feature is the round tower of St Mary's church. Almost unknown in other parts of England, there are 168 such structures in East Anglia, of which this is one of the score or so shown by the features known as blind arcading and other architectural details, to be of Anglo-Saxon date.

NORWICH Norfolk
TG 235085 OS 134
Norwich is the principal town in Norfolk. The castle, built about 1160 and refaced with fresh stone in the nineteenth century, houses a splendid museum in which relics from Caistor St Edmund and many other places are exhibited. The traveller staying in or visiting Norwich before setting out on the Progress will find no lack of interest besides the Castle Museum. There is the cathedral, and there are thirty-two other medieval churches. These include St Mary Coslany, reputedly the oldest church in the county, and St Peter Hungate, in Princes Street, which is a museum of ecclesiastical art and East Anglian antiquities.

CAISTOR St EDMUND Norfolk
TG 232034 OS 134
Caistor St Edmund is three miles south of the centre of Norwich by way of a minor road that runs beside the east bank of the River Tas. Ten years after Boudicca's defeat the Roman authorities sited a new capital for the Iceni here, Venta Icenorum, five miles down stream from Tasburgh. They also had a metalled road built along the route from here to Colchester, starting on the west bank of the River Tas, opposite the new town. For thirty miles of its length this road is now the A140.

The remaining bank and ditch by the parish church on the outskirts of Caistor St Edmund, mark one of Venta Icenorum's four boundaries

Landscape by a tributary of the River Waveney near Scole

LONG STRATTON Norfolk
TM 196924 OS 134

Long Stratton is two miles south of Tasburgh, on the A140. One of only two surviving sexton's wheels of fifteenth-century date has been preserved in St Mary's church. This is a device for determining when the day of the Lady Feast comes round, a voluntary movable feast kept over a cycle of seven years.

SCOLE Norfolk
TM 150790 OS 156

Scole is ten miles south of Long Stratton on the A140, at the crossing of the River Waveney which here forms the Norfolk-Suffolk border and, in all likelihood, was also the boundary between the Iceni on the north and the Trinovantes on the south. This was probably where the hostelry named Villa Faustina *in the Antonine Itinerary (a Roman road-book compiled in about the year A.D. 200) was located.*

TIVETSHALL St MARGARET Norfolk
TM 163871 OS 156

The village is reached by turning west off the A140 four miles south of Long Stratton on to the B1134, and turning left off this in less than one mile. In the church is "a prodigiously large Royal Arms of Queen Elisabeth I – a most remarkable survival" (Pevsner).

DICKLEBURGH Norfolk
TM 167824 OS 156

Dickleburgh is three miles down the A140 from where the B1134 turns off to Tivetshall St Margaret. The large All Saints church, mostly of about 1300, contains many interesting features, including a fine Royal Arms dated 1662, when King Charles II was newly restored.

LITTLE STONHAM Suffolk
TM 119605 OS 155

The village lies just west of the A140 half a mile north of the point where this and the A1120 cross. The Magpie Inn is on the A140, at the map reference. The stony ground implied in the first part of the name could have been the core of the Roman road.

Castle, the new town, *Durnovaria* (Dorchester) is a similar distance away; at Wroxeter in Shropshire, to cite another, *Viroconium* was laid out on the plain three and half miles west of the old Cornovian centre on the Wrekin.

There is a direct route, forty-five miles in length, from Tasburgh south to Colchester, which today starts as the A140. We can imagine Boudicca and her Icenian army moving off along this route on a day in the late summer of the year 60. Tasburgh lies near the southern limit of what is, for Norfolk, almost hilly countryside – the land rises to as much as 225 feet above sea-level at a point two miles east of Caistor St Edmund. The landscape is well wooded today, this district being particularly noted for the size of the holly trees. But early in the first century, the forests were much more extensive, and cleared ground was less in evidence. Such undulations as there are in the neighbourhood of Tasburgh, however, soon give way, in the vicinity of **Long Stratton**, to the characteristic East Anglian level ground, featureless except for the occasional shallow valley.

After twelve miles on the march the Icenians came down the gentle slope to the crossing of the River Waveney, at **Scole**. Today, the traveller passes near villages such as **Tivetshall St Margaret**, or through them, as **Dickleburgh**, on the way; but these are for the most part Saxon foundations, springing up as forest was cleared in early medieval times.

Here at Scole, seventeen miles east of Thetford along the open valley, was an opportunity for Boudicca's allies from the west to join her – Coritani, Cornovii, Dobunnni, Durotriges; and some Brigantes from farther north. The Catuvellauni, like the Trinovantes, would join her nearer Colchester, to avoid increasing their journey. Scole was a place of some importance in those days, with a settlement and a wharf beside the river.

From the crossing of the River Waveney the increased army carried on south, for seventeen miles, to the next important crossing, that of the River Gipping. This stretch of the road, crossing level ground once afforested but now occupied by extensive farms, is known locally as the Pye Road, after the Magpie Inn at **Little Stonham**, three quarters of a mile north of the crossing of Boudicca's route by the Saxmundham–Stowmarket road, the A1120. Just north of the Magpie the modern road lies a little west of the romanised route, but a stretch of the mound (or *agger*) of this can still be distinguished in the field to the east.

There was another settlement beside the crossing of the River Gipping, at **Baylham**. Round here the old route is somewhat obscured by the railway and modern roads. But after a while it can be followed more easily once again, now on the A1100, to the junction of this with the modernised A12(T), which then represents the route taken by Boudicca almost all the way into **Colchester**.

Approaching the town from the north, the forces under Boudicca's command crossed the River Colne to find the town without walls or other obstacles to deter violent entry. The Britons swarmed in, sacking shops and houses and stores of merchandise, and slaughtering their enemies, and the friends of their enemies, with abandon. A picked band concentrated on the great temple of Claudius, focal point of British detestation. The defenders held out for two days before succumbing – perhaps after they

BAYLHAM Suffolk
TM 105515 OS 155

Baylham village is six miles north-west of Ipswich, just west of the B1113. The traveller on the A140 from Scole can take the B1078 west from where the A140 joins the A45(T) to Needham Market, and then go south on the B1113. The settlement of the Trinovantes known as Combretovium was one mile to the east of the village, on the far side of the River Gipping at Baylham House farm. The bridge over the river here marks the vicinity of where Boudicca and her army crossed in 60 A.D.

COLCHESTER Essex
TL 998253 OS 168

Colchester, the principal town in Essex, is fifty miles north-east of London by the A12(T). The best-preserved building of the Romano-British period is the west gate, the Balkerne Gate, of third-century date. A local delicacy which the traveller should not miss is the steak, kidney and oyster pie.

Top, the mill and bridge on the River Gipping are within one mile of Baylham village. Above, the Balkerne Gate in Colchester's well-reserved Roman wall

MARKS TEY Essex
TL 911238 OS 168
Marks Tey is five miles west-south-west of Colchester by the A12(T). The church with the rare wooden font is a quarter of a mile north-west of the point where the Roman road from Colchester to St Albans, Stane Street (A120) leaves the Colchester–London road (A12(T)).

KELVEDON Essex
TL 861186 OS 168
Kelvedon is ten miles south-west of Colchester by the A12(T) which passes by the village on the south-east.

WITHAM Essex
TL 816153 OS 168
Witham is four miles south-west of Kelvedon on the A12(T) which, as at Kelvedon, passes it by one the south-east.

CHELMSFORD Essex
TL 705070 OS 167
Chelmsford is twenty-two miles south-west of Colchester on the A12(T). It bore the pretentious name Caesaromagus, *"Caesar's Market", which on the face of it would presuppose a large and important town – such as* Caesaromagus, *capital of the Belgic Celtic tribe, the Bellovaci, now Beauvais, Oise, France. It has been suggested that the administrators of Roman Britain wished to establish the Trinovantes in a new tribal centre, and that construction of a suitably large-scale town had just begun when Boudicca, together with her Trinovantian allies, made her thrust to expel the invaders. When this failed there was no more talk of a grand town, but the name survived, attached to the ordinary small town and the military fort which once existed in what is now the south part of Chelmsford.*

LONDON
TQ 330810 OS 177
Shortly after Boudicca's destruction of undefended Londinium in A.D. 60, a new start was made on a forum and basilica and other buildings, which have been located beneath Leadenhall Market. This is in the area bounded by Gracechurch, Fenchurch and Leadenhall Streets, at the above map reference, a quarter of a mile north-north-east of the north end of London Bridge. It is probable that the work started in about A.D. 75 was on the site of some at least of the buildings destroyed by Boudicca.

In the mid-nineteenth century Prince Albert suggested that the sculptor Thomas Thorneycroft should undertake a major work of sculpture on the ever-popular theme of Boadicea, as the Icenian queen was then known. By 1864 Thorneycroft was able to exhibit "Colossal Head of

had heard that a hoped-for relief force of the Ninth Legion, marching from Longthorpe near Peterborough, had been utterly routed by the Britons. Today the traveller can still see the basal structure of the temple, preserved both by its massive construction and by its having been re-used a thousand years later as the foundation of the castle built by the Normans. This is now the Castle Museum, in which a most important exhibition of local archaeological material can be seen.

Whatever else she might be going to achieve, Boudicca would never again have quite the satisfaction she now felt as she gazed on the obliterated town.

This had been founded in A.D. 48–49, as a military colony near *Camulodunum* (formerly the seat of the British king Cunobelin, Shakespeare's Cymbeline) "to act as a support against rebels, and to instruct the allies in the duties enjoined by the laws". The new colony stood for urban civilisation, the hallmark of Roman culture; and was the centre of the cult of the deified emperor Claudius, the focus of provincial loyalties. Beside the temple were a theatre and the senate house, an impressive cultural complex. Roman veterans formed the core of the population, but there were also administrators, merchants and some Britons. The veterans were undesirable people in the main, arrogant, stern and selfish. Their land was granted to them from the conquered domains of the local British royal house and "They kept driving the Britons off their lands, calling them prisoners and slaves" – which, in fact, according to Roman law, they were. In destroying this nest of the most evil of the oppressors of her people and of the neighbouring British tribes, Boudicca had made real their wildest dreams.

Boudicca and her army left the ruins of Colchester to the scavengers, and began the fifty-mile march to London. The endless level landscapes of her home were now replaced by a somewhat more hilly terrain – afforested, of course, but with more frequent clearings and farmsteads. Today the traveller passes through **Marks Tey**, and would do well not to pass without having a look at the remarkable fifteenth-century wooden font in the church. Two of the doors and one window here are shaped with "Roman" bricks, made by some British worker in the near by brickfields.

Ten miles from Colchester Boudicca came to **Kelvedon**, where the Trinovantes had a substantial settlement between Brockwell Lane and the River Blackwater, in the south part of the little modern town. The Roman army had built a fort alongside the British settlement, south-east of the present High Street, but this had probably been abandoned before Boudicca came that way.

Four miles further on the traveller can pass by the town of **Witham** or pay it a brief visit, to see the church on the hill known as Chipping Hill ("Market Hill") in which once again Norman builders used "Roman" bricks in their arches.

Eight miles beyond Witham is **Chelmsford**, where Boudicca's all-conquering army destroyed a Roman fort, which stood in what is now the south part of the town, on the right bank of the River Can, in the vicinity of Moulsham Street. The Chelmsford and Essex Museum in Oaklands Park contains collections of local archaeological material as well as many other interesting exhibits.

Nothing intervened over the next thirty miles to protect the budding city of *Londinium* from the avengers. Moving today along this route, which was called Hare Street in medieval times, the traveller begins to lose sight of the countryside when only half way along from Chelmsford, and to plunge into the seemingly endless conurbation of **London** – descendant of the little ten-year-old embryo which, nineteen hundred and more years ago, Boudicca's army found open to assault, without defences and without defenders. For the Governor Suetonius, having pushed on to the relief of London with a small force of cavalry, had decided that it was indefensible and again withdrawn north-westwards, "allowing those citizens fit to do so to join his column." Only the poor and infirm – "women or feeble old men unfit for war" – were therefore left to face the Britons' wrath. One of the buildings destroyed was the residence of the hated Procurator of Britain – who had fled to Gaul. If this was on the same site as that of the Governor's dwelling in the ensuing reconstruction, then it was where Cannon Street station is today.

Destruction was swift and comprehensive, and it is no wonder that nothing remained standing of pre-Boudiccan London. Such relics as have been salvaged from the catastrophe, as well as those from later periods, can be seen to great advantage in the Museum of London (located in the Barbican Centre) and in the British Museum.

Well pleased with their successes, the army of Boudicca now turned north-west to the romanised city, *Verulamium*, then beginning to develop beside the River Ver at St Albans. The traveller tracing Boudicca's course must go west from the City of London to Marble Arch, and then turn north-west up the Edgware Road (A5), the start of Watling Street. This runs straight for ten miles to the high ground at **Brockley Hill**, where the road veers north-east for one mile, crosses over the M1 and through the A41(T), and turns back to run north-north-east for eight miles to **St Albans**.

Here again, Boudicca found few defences or defenders to protect the people and buildings. Shops and dwellings had grown up beside Watling Street, though many people were still living in the old Catuvellaunian settlement now known as Prae Wood, immediately to the west of the new town. The wood so named, the site of part of the important pre-Roman community, lies to the north of the A414 Hemel Hempstead–St Albans road for a mile on the St Albans side (the east side) of the M10. The other part of the pre-Roman town was immediately north of Prae Wood, at Gorhambury.

The traveller getting to *Verulamium* along Watling Street (A5) crosses junction 1 of the M10 and keeps on for a further half mile. Then, north of the junction of the A5 with the A412, Watling Street enters *Verulamium* as a footpath; the traveller takes a minor road for three quarters of a mile to the A414, and then turns right into *Verulamium*. The museum, on a site in the post-Boudiccan town, houses material from both the British and the Romano-British periods. Other important exhibits are on display at the St Albans City museum, in Hatfield Road.

Boudicca now received the grave news that the Roman commander Suetonius had gathered what troops he could, and was coming along

Boadicea, part of a chariot group now in progress" at the Royal Academy Exhibition.

The Prince followed the progress of the work with interest, lending white horses from the Royal Mews as models, and offering to find an appropriate site for the completed group. However, the Prince died before the work was complete; and when it was, it was to stand for years in the sculptor's studio in Wilton Place until, in 1885, Thorneycroft died.

It so happened that a few years later, excavations were started on the tumulus in Parliament Hill Fields, Highgate (TQ 274865), traditionally known as Boadicea's Grave. Meanwhile the sculptor's son, John Thorneycroft, offered to present the group to the public, and to contribute towards the cost of casting it – with the Parliament Hill tumulus as a probable site.

However, after debate a more appropriate place was selected, on the north side of the west end of Westminster Bridge near its junction with the Victoria Embankment, just opposite the Houses of Parliament. Cast in bronze and partly paid for by public subscription, the group was erected in 1902 on a pedestal provided by the local authority, the London County Council. And there Boadicea – with the amendment BOUDICCA also appearing – stands in her chariot, the personification of the Victory which finally eluded her. When the work was done there was little enough knowledge of what a Celtic war chariot looked like, though Caesar does give a graphic description. The sculptor preferred the "armoured milk-float" design. Nevertheless, the dramatic group attests the popular regard in which the Icenian warrior queen was, and is, held.

BROCKLEY HILL Greater London
TQ 175940 OS 176
The A5(T) passes over Brockley Hill one mile north-west of the junction with the A410, between Edgware and Stanmore. A pottery named Sulloniacae was producing here in Romano-British times. An obelisk recording it is in the grounds of the Royal National Orthopaedic Hospital, on the west side of the road.

St ALBANS Hertfordshire
TL 135073 OS 166
St Albans city is four miles north-east of junction 6 of the M1, by way of the A412. The Verulamium Museum, St Martin's, is within the post-Boudiccan Romano-British town, Verulamium, one mile west of the city centre, on the A414. Parts of St Michael's church were built of Romano-British brick in the tenth century, one hundred years before the Norman Conquest.

The Roman theatre of Verulamium

St Michael's church is close to the
Verulamium Museum in St Albans

The River Ouzel on the southern
outskirts of Fenny Stratford bordered
the settlement known as Magiovinium

Part of the town wall of Roman Lactodorum was discovered by the stream at the back of the churchyard in the centre of Towcester

DUNSTABLE Bedfordshire
TL 018218 OS 166
Dunstable is twelve miles north-west of St
Albans on the A5(T). The Romano-British
settlement, Durocobrivis, was in the south-
west part of the town, in the angle formed
by Watling Street and West Street, which
is on the line of the very ancient route, the
Icknield Way. Archaeological finds from
Dunstable and elsewhere in Bedfordshire
can be seen in the Museum and Art
Gallery, Wardown Park, Luton, four and
half miles to the east.

FENNY STRATFORD Buckinghamshire
SP 887339 OS 165
The Romano-British town Magiovinium
was near the right bank of the River Ouzel
just south-east of the old bridge carrying
Watling Street into Fenny Stratford. It was
in the triangle formed by Watling Street,
the by-pass and the railway, on property
named Dropshort, by which name the
place is known in many books of
reference. Fenny Stratford has been
absorbed by Bletchley; but the traveller
who visits St Martin's church will see the
Fenny Poppers, small cannon which are
fired on St Martin's day, the 11th of
November.

STONY STRATFORD Buckinghamshire
SP 785405 OS 152
The village, now by-passed, is seven miles
northwest of Fenny Stratford on the
A5(T). Old Stratford is on the opposite
bank of the River Great Ouse, a quarter of
a mile further on. Like so many once
independent and unspoiled villages and
small towns, these Stratfords are suffering
a reduction in their identity by the
encroachment of the extensive "new
town" which bears the name of another
such engulfed village – Milton Keynes.

TOWCESTER Northamptonshire
SP 692488 OS 152
Towcester is at the crossing of the A5(T)
and the A43(T), eight miles north-west of
Stony Stratford. The Catuvellaunian
settlement here became the walled town
Lactodorum.

NORTON Northamptonshire
SP 602638 OS 152
Norton is eleven miles north-west of
Towcester, half a mile west of the A5(T) by
a secondary road. The settlement
Bannaventa, *which was later developed*
into a walled town, was near Whilton
Lodge, half a mile north-east of the village.

Watling Street from the north-west, to offer her battle. Her decision to conduct an uprising against well-disciplined Roman soldiers had been no light one. Success had somewhat reconciled the queen and her principal adherents to the risk; and now that what must be the final battle was in the offing, the Britons faced it with a will.

Suetonius Paulinus was a brilliant military commander, with a fine record, when he came to Britain in A.D. 58 He had been trained in mountain warfare, and this would suit him well in his campaigns in western Britain, among the fierce tribes in Wales. However, he was over sixty years of age when he arrived in Britain – in excellent health and spirits, but hardly flexible in ideas.

Occupied with his problems in north Wales, Suetonius had made an error that was almost to cost him Britain. He left the simmering unrest, the imminent insurrection, to subordinate officers, believing that the fierce tribes and the Druids, in north Wales and on Anglesey, offered the more urgent threat. For there, the native British power was still dauntingly strong and Suetonius Paulinus was determined to master it. The Snowdon mountains provided natural protection for the rich granary of Mon – Anglesey – "thickly populated, and a safe retreat for fugitives": and anti-Roman elements from all over Britain had in fact gathered here under the protective aegis of the Druids, whose great religious centre Anglesey was.

Boudicca's route was clear – it was Watling Street all the way, a route which can be followed by the traveller today. First, some fifteen miles northwest of *Verulamium*, to **Dunstable**, where there was a British settlement known later, and possibly then, as *Durocobrivis*. Twelve miles further on, at **Fenny Stratford**, at the crossing of the River Ouzel, there was another such settlement, *Magiovinium*, just east of the river. Eight miles further yet, some thirty miles from *Verulamium*, Boudicca crossed the River Great Ouse at **Stony Stratford**. Then on for another straight march to the crossing of the River Tove at **Towcester**, where, in after years, there was a walled town called *Lactodurum*, a small settlement when Boudicca passed that way.

A little more than ten miles on, the British came to a minor road junction at **Norton**, where there was a settlement, *Bannaventa*. The same distance again took them to the low ground between the Rivers Avon and Swift, where there was a settlement aptly named *Tripontium*, "Three Bridges". This is to the west of Watling Street, just north of where the present road runs under the M6 at Caves Inn farm, **Churchover**.

Boudicca had now come sixty miles from *Verulamium*. Suetonius was somewhere ahead on a collision course, and she increased her forward scouting, to avoid being taken unawares. Over undulating country the host moved on for seven miles, to **High Cross**, where Watling Street crosses that other great Roman artery, the Fosse Way. There was a small Coritanian settlement here; when the Romans later built a fort beside it, they named it *Venonis*.

Now the two armies could not be far apart. For ten more miles the road continued through woodland and open country until, beside the River Anker, the watch-towers and smoke of the Roman fort *Manduessedum*, now **Mancetter**, came into view. It has been persuasively argued that it was here that Suetonius chose a battleground and awaited Boudicca's attack. He knew he was greatly outnumbered, but he relied on the iron discipline and well-practiced tactics of the Roman army to see him through. The Roman soldiers sustained the first wild charge of the Britons, and then with increasing mastery stemmed the attack and turned it to defeat. The sweet taste of the day was spoiled for Suetonius in that Boudicca escaped. But for the British queen there was to be no second chance, as she knew. She returned to her native land and died, deeply mourned by her countrymen and buried, it is said, in a manner suited to so mighty and courageous a woman.

CHURCHOVER Warwickshire
SP 510808 OS 140
Churchover village is one mile west of the junction of the A5(T) and A426 roads, twelve miles north-west of Norton. The settlement, and later walled town, Tripontium (known in books of reference as Cave's Inn from the place of that name) was situated a mile and a half south-east of the village, between Watling Street and the grounds of Coton Hall.

HIGH CROSS Leicestershire
SP 473886 OS 140
High Cross is six miles north-west of Churchover on the A5(T).

MANCETTER Warwickshire
SP 320966 OS 140
Mancetter is just south of the A5(T) at the south-east end of Atherstone, eleven miles north-west of High Cross. The Roman fort, Manduessedum, was on the east bank of the River Anker, at the junction with Watling Street of a road to Leicester. It has been considered likely that the battleground described by Tacitus could have been on the lower slopes of the ridge between Nuneaton and Atherstone – for example, on Camp Hill, a mile and a half north-west of Nuneaton on the A47(T). This site is two miles south of Manduessedum, and a mile and a half in a direct line at right angles to the nearest point on Watling Street.

The round tower of St Mary's, Tasburgh

Alfred the Great
A journey from disaster to triumph
CHIPPENHAM–WEDMORE 878

Anne Ross

Alfred (849–99) was born at Wantage (Berkshire), youngest of the five sons of Aethelwulf (d. 858), king of the southern kingdom of Wessex. When Alfred succeeded to the throne in 871, Wessex was threatened by the Viking invasions engulfing the other Anglo-Saxon kingdoms. In 878 Alfred was beaten by the Danish king Guthrum at Chippenham, but he managed to bounce back, winning decisively at Edington. Guthrum accepted baptism and the Danes withdrew to East Anglia. Alfred was to extend his control into the Midlands kingdom of Mercia and in 886 he captured London. By treaty with him, Guthrum acknowledged the limitation of Danish settlement to what was to be known as the Danelaw. Alfred's military reorganisation enabled the English to withstand a new wave of Viking invasions (893–96).

The chief surviving historical writings of the period, written to glorify the House of Wessex, idealise Alfred. But besides being a cunning and ferocious warleader and a shrewd politician, he was clearly a pious man with a devout view of the purposes of his royal office. This was reflected in his codification of the laws and in his efforts to revive Latin learning. Alfred is unusual among medieval kings in having engaged in literary composition. He can plausibly be regarded as the founder of the kingship of England, which was to be built up in the forty years after his death by his son Edward the Elder and his grandson Athelstan. Alfred was buried in the New Minster (Hyde Abbey) at Winchester.

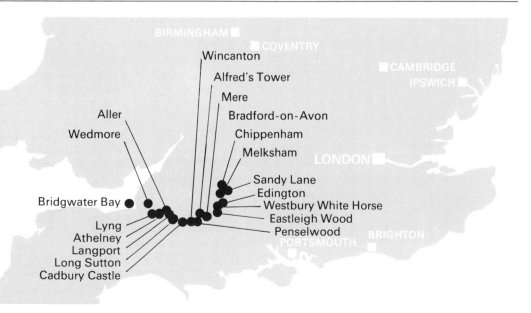

In an age when men of outstanding character were guiding the warring nations of Europe towards settlement and peace, in a period recognised as an Heroic Age, King Alfred the Great earned his illustrious title as much in seats of learning as on the battlefield, by diplomacy as much as by force of arms. Himself suffering from a physical disability, he succeeded to the rule of the Kingdom of Wessex at a time when Viking invasions were disrupting rural and urban life, retarding the development of Hiberno-Saxon art and learning, and hazarding the whole future of burgeoning Christianity.

Alfred's principles, together with the essential element of good fortune, carried Wessex through the danger of imminent obliteration, and thereby the entire nation towards security. Today, it may not be easy to conceive of the strength of a man who, having the position and the ability to lead men to fight, never himself failed in his devotion to duty and his religious beliefs; who was untiring in seeking out ways of making and keeping peace; and who wisely ruled friend and former foe alike. A man of his word, to whom an oath was binding and sacred, he had a personal purity and self-abnegation to back the strong arm bearing the avenging sword — attributes rare at any time, but then virtually unparalleled.

In spite of the great difficulties with which he was confronted, and the many undertakings which demanded his constant attention, Alfred succeeded in initiating a programme for the translation into English of certain books "which are the most necessary for all men to know". He created a realm which was sufficiently stable, in unstable times, to permit the growth of all the Hiberno-Saxon arts and learning, and to provide a milieu in which the Christian faith could take on a new depth and meaning and dignity. The reign of King Alfred, then, is one of the most inspiring periods in the history of the English-speaking world, during which the kingdom of Wessex was snatched from the very brink of decisive and irreversible Viking conquest. The events which took place during his reign were to lead, ultimately, to the political unification of England.

Little enough might have been known of this man who flourished eleven hundred years ago, had it not been that Bishop Asser, a Welsh divine, compiled a detailed and vivid record of Alfred's life, and that copies of this have survived. Among the many books produced by scholars who have translated and annotated this work in the course of recent centuries, one of the most informative and readable is the work of Keynes and Lapidge (1983) cited in the bibliography. The reader will find in this, at greater length, an account of the events of Alfred's life that are recorded here.

Alfred, the fifth and youngest son of King Aethelwulf of Wessex and his first wife, the noble and religious Osburh, was born in 849 at Wantage (then in Berkshire, now in Oxfordshire), one of the royal residences of the kings of this period. Today, a splendid statue in the market-place commemorates the Saxon king, while a field at the top of the town is known, according to local tradition, as Alfred's Meadow. In his early years Alfred moved with his family from residence to residence, deriving his education both from what he observed and from what his parents and tutors taught him. While yet a boy, Alfred memorised poems, psalms and prayers, true to the innate tradition of oral learning which was strong then among the Anglo-Saxons as it was, and still is, in Celtic societies. Alfred early laid the foundations of the spiritual life that was to represent so important a facet of his character in later years. He went to Rome when he was four, and again two years later, this time shortly after the death of his mother. On the second visit he accompanied his father, who then met Judith, daughter of Charles the Bald, King of the Franks, when the English party stayed at the royal residence on their journey to Rome. On the return journey Aethelwulf and Judith were married at "Verberie" (possibly Vervins (Aisne), forty miles north of Rheims) by Hincmar, Bishop of Rheims.

One result of his early travels was Alfred's lasting devotion to the Papal See, as attested by his painstaking translation of Pope Gregory's "*Pastoral Care*", in which Alfred acknowledges the help of Asser, "my bishop". Another result, this time of his journey to the court of King Charles, may have been the interest he took in later years in Frankish scholarship and learning, and in Frankish tactics against the ever-present threat of the vicious Viking raiders.

Asser said of the young Alfred that he was loved not only by his father and his mother, but by all people, above all by his brothers; and that he was educated entirely at the court of the king. "As he advanced through the years of infancy and youth, his form appeared more comely than that of his brothers; in looks, speech and manners he was more graceful, more gracious than they." Although he enjoyed the company of churchmen, among whom he spent much of his time, and favoured academic pursuits, he was also vigorous and active, and became a fine huntsman and a courageous warrior. Asser further describes him as a zealot of hunting in all its branches, who hunted with great assiduity and success. This he justified by pointing out that skill and good fortune in this art, as in all other activities, are among the gifts of God.

Asser, whose Hebraic name was in all probability a version of the Celtic word of the same meaning, *gwyn* ("fair, pure") became Bishop of Sherborne, one of the Wessex Sees. His praise of the king is unstinted and sincere, and very Welsh. His account is impressively substantiated in documents such as the *Anglo-Saxon Chronicle*, (which was begun in Alfred's time in the manner of the Frankish annals) and in the evidence of recent archaeological research.

When Alfred was nineteen, three years before he became king, he married Ealhswith, whose mother was of the royal house of Mercia (in the English Midlands) and whose father was a Mercian noble, a man of high rank. We can be sure that the political implications of such a union would be to the mutual advantage of the two kingdoms. Alfred and Ealhswith had five children, three girls and two boys: the elder boy, Edward, was to rule Wessex for a quarter of a century, from the death of his father to 924.

Alfred had been taking a leading part in the defence of Wessex before, at Easter 871, he succeeded to the high command and the kingship on the death of his brother Aethelred. He now bore the whole burden of opposing two Viking armies, ending an inconclusive fight at Wilton, Wiltshire, by bargaining for an uneasy and temporary truce. Alfred had to follow a similar course again in 876 and again in 877, only to find that the daunting menace recurred in the following year. By now, however, he and his subjects knew and understood each other, to the great advantage of the country. After a period of skirmishing and preparation, the king and a sufficient number of his men were able to mount and sustain a campaign which culminated in what was at last an effective victory over the Northmen, in the summer of 878, at Edington, Wiltshire (Ethandun). And although both Alfred himself and his successors were to endure many further dangers and threats before the Kingdom of England was finally established, the victory achieved that day was to be ultimately decisive.

This is the route, the progress to victory, taken by King Alfred at that turbulent time.

After protracted negotiations, treaties and settlements, Alfred hoped he had seen the last of the Vikings in Wessex for the time being, and felt confident enough to spend Christmas 877 at or near Chippenham. Very early in the New Year (878), however, the Vikings appeared entirely unheralded at Chippenham, utterly surprising the king who had received no intelligence of their movements. The Vikings raided extensively in Wessex, dispersing some of the people and establishing their rule over the rest. But they did not succeed in capturing the king, which would have been fatal for England in general and for Wessex in particular. For Alfred was able to make a rapid and secret departure, with a very few adherents, to establish a base in the West Country, beyond Selwood and beyond the Somerset marshes.

"The West Country" – words which evoke at once King Arthur the Briton and King Alfred the Anglo-Saxon. In spite of conflicting traditions, this part of Britain is as much the kingdom of Arthur as it is that of Alfred. In the beautiful, contrasting counties of the West Country the peoples who had survived Arthur's wars rose anew and, in union with the newcomers, formed the British people of Wessex. Celt and Saxon in combination, they were to attain glory under their natural leader, Alfred, who seven hundred years after his death, was to be accorded the title Great by the acclamation of the descendants of his own people.

Asser and the writer of the *Anglo-Saxon Chronicle*, between them, convey a graphic picture of the plight of the fugitives, and of how they fared during the ensuing five months. At first, in the weeks of wintry weather towards the end of the farming year, supplies of any kind were hard to come by, and to subsist at all the king and his band had to rely on incessant raids into territory under Viking control. From this disastrous starting point, as the days drew out and the sun passed the spring equinox, so gradually and inexorably the king developed the resolution and the purpose to reverse the course of events and regain the initiative. The king and his men, safe within the protection of the marshes in that momentous spring of 878, together planned to overcome the ship-borne raiders.

Until drainage was undertaken in medieval days, the low-lying marshes and fens now known as the Somerset Levels were for most of the year a marsh, dotted with "islands" and ridges, dominated to the east by Glastonbury Tor, once crowned by a Celtic hillfort, later by a church. The uninspiring character of the Levels in the late winter was to some extent deceptive, insofar as it seemed to imply a barren waste. For, as Alfred knew, there was always a harvest of fish and water-fowl for the taking and, in the summer, the "islands", accessible when receding waters laid bare ancient tracks and causeways, afforded excellent pasture for winter-starved

*Athelney Hill is one mile east of Lyng, on
the A361, eight miles east-north-east of
Taunton. In 1801 the landlord erected a
monument on the hill to perpetuate the
memory of King Alfred. (At this period, the
date of King Alfred's campaigns based on
Athelney was thought to have been 879, as
in the inscription.)*

LYNG Somerset
ST 333290 OS 193
*Lyng is seven miles east-north-east of
Taunton on the A361.*

flocks and herds. All the region round the higher features lies below, or only slightly above, sea-level. The frequent, age-long flooding by languid rivers has encouraged the development here and there of peat, and the growth of rushes, reeds and alders. It is popularly supposed that the Saxon word *Somersaetas* (from which "Somerset" derives) had the meaning "summer dwellers" – a reference to a people who, like crofters in mountainous regions, moved with their beasts to the summer marshland pastures. It is more probable, however, that the word denotes a people living within the area administered from Somerton (the seat of local government in those days) on the River Cary, seven miles south of Glastonbury on the B3151.

The twelfth-century chronicler William of Malmesbury wrote of **Athelney** that it was "not an island in the sea, but so inaccessible on account of bogs and inundation of lakes that it cannot be approached except by boat". The Alfred Stone, overlooking Athelney Farm, reminds today's traveller of the identity of the place where King Alfred extended the monastery, later to be known as Athelney Abbey. Nearby is the "island" of **Lyng**, site of another of Alfred's fortifications. Like Athelney, to which it was connected by some sort of causeway, Lyng rises high and dry above the marshland. Today, Lyng is a small village, linked by road to Athelney, itself now marked only by a single farm.

It was in drained land near the margin of the Levels, two or three miles west-north-west of Athelney at Newton Park, North Petherton, that by the luckiest chance imaginable a golden ornament was dug out of the ground in 1693. Again, by the best of good fortune, it came to rest in the Ashmolean Museum, Oxford. There can be no doubt that here we have an object made for King Alfred, for his own use or for him to bestow as a princely gift.

Two and a half inches long, the "jewel" consists of an oval "body", round at one end and pointed at the other, and a stem or terminal. The front of the body bears the figure of a man holding two sceptres of similar design, the outlines of man and sceptres being in gold, and the spaces filled with coloured enamels. The back is formed by a gold plate carved with a simplified design of smooth foliage, the contrasting background filled with basket hatching. Round the edge of the body is a row of capital letters, forming the words AELFRED MEC HEHT GEWYRCAN (which translate "Alfred ordered me to be be made"). The stem or terminal takes the form of an elaborately decorated head of an animal, with curved horns, long ears, and round eyes, and with a wide mouth holding a short, slightly flattened tube.

Examination of illustrations in contemporary manuscripts seems to confirm the deduction that this tube may originally have held a narrow "blade" of ivory, bone or wood, used for marking the place in a book and for aiding the eye to follow the written line. Another suggestion, that the "jewel" might have formed the terminal of a staff or sceptre, or wand of office, requires substantiation.

From Athelney (*Aethelingaig*, "island of princes"), then, King Alfred would move out from time to time, before and after Easter (which this year fell on the 23rd of March) to join in skirmishes and petty engagements with elements of the Viking armies. When not so employed, Alfred remained in retreat, in meditation and prayer. And it is from these few weeks – which must have seemed interminable to the beleaguered king – that so many

Access to the Alfred monument is invited via Athelney Farm, seen here over the brow of the hill

tales have survived about Alfred – tales which have passed into the unpredictable popular repertoire to stand alongside the legend of King Cnut and the waves of Southampton Water, or of King John losing his baggage in the Wash. The best-known Alfred story is, of course, the one about the cakes.

The king is alleged to have sheltered one day under the welcome if humble roof of a swineherd's dwelling. Sitting keeping warm by the fire, he was lost in profound reverie, and failed to notice that the cakes or loaves the herd's wife was baking by the fire were burning. The woman, not realising the exalted status of her handsome young guest, attacked him with reproaches and, some say, a box on the ears. A simple story, to illustrate the depths of the king's distraction of mind and the humiliation of his circumstances at this time.

This tale did not apparently become current until after Alfred's death, and it does not figure in the works of Asser or of William of Malmesbury. William did, however, introduce or repeat tales about the miraculous intervention of certain saints on behalf of the king, and he also tells a story of how King Alfred disguised himself as a minstrel and so wandered singing into the Viking camp with a friend, there gathering information about the enemy's plans. He then returned to Athelney, described his exploit, and used the information he had gained to assist him in preparing a plan of campaign against the Vikings.

Alfred spent part of his time during April overseeing the completion of his defences on Athelney Hill where, presumably, he kept his wife and family in safety, with such possessions as he had by him. But this must also have been a time of making contact with men of influence throughout Wessex, and for formulating plans of action. When Alfred eventually set off, early in May, his intention was to collect enough men to overpower the Vikings, and to bring the enemy to battle forthwith: and whether he or someone else had secured the information, he must have been certain that he was not going off on a wild goose chase. The fact that he was joined as he went along by men organised and prepared for marching and fighting, moreover, implies that solid preparations must have been made during the fateful month of April. News of what was afoot penetrated through Somerset and Wiltshire, and as far as Hampshire, some sixty miles as the crow flies east of Athelney, to be greeted with determined anticipation by men who believed in their king's qualitities and his capacity to succeed.

Early in May, then, King Alfred left the shelter of Athelney and the Levels, and set out along the western stretch of the ancient track connecting the West Country and Kent. Taking a last look back over the marshes towards **Bridgwater Bay**, he soon reached **Langport** and, with his nucleus of a host behind him, made his way eastwards, up the valley of the River Yeo, past **Long Sutton**. Four and a half miles further on, the old route is crossed by another ancient track, the once-romanised Fosse Way, which King Alfred could see as it pointed north-north-east towards parts of his land where the Danes had raided so freely, and south-south-west to countryside which he had cleared of them.

Six miles more, and the king could see, rising from the valley one mile to the south, the great ruined defences of **Cadbury Castle**, derelict for

BRIDGWATER BAY Somerset
SS 280500 OS 182
Bridgwater Bay is at the head of the Bristol Channel, between Minehead and Weston-super-Mare.

LANGPORT Somerset
ST 422267 OS 193
Langport is on the A372, three miles west of Long Sutton. Another hilltop site like Athelney and Lyng, it was the last of a chain of small Devon and Somerset Saxon forts.

LONG SUTTON Somerset
ST 469253 OS 193
Long Sutton lies just south of the A372, three miles east of Langport. Among the other buildings of interest is a Friends Meeting House of 1717.

CADBURY CASTLE Somerset
ST 628252 OS 183
This famous hillfort at South Cadbury is six miles west of Wincanton, just south of the A303(T). The hill was first occupied by people of the Stone Age, about 4,000 B.C.; it remained in occupation intermittently until the reign of King John, A.D. 1200. A full and fascinating account of the place is Leslie Alcock's "By South Cadbury is that Camelot", published by Thames and Hudson in 1972.

WINCANTON Somerset
ST 713285 OS 183
Wincanton is seven miles west of Mere on the A303(T). Numerous handsome houses of the seventeenth, eighteenth and nineteenth centuries survive in the town.

PENSELWOOD Somerset
ST 756314 OS 183
Penselwood is situated one mile up a minor road leading north off the A303(T) three miles east of Wincanton. Although the place is mentioned in the Anglo-Saxon Chronicle under the year 658, no traces of Anglo-Saxon work have been recorded in the church of St Michael, in which the south door and the font are of the Norman period.

Opposite top, Burrow Mump is another "island" in the Somerset Levels having strong associations with King Alfred
below, the grassy shore of Bridgwater Bay near Steart

ALFRED'S TOWER Wiltshire
ST 745350 OS 183
Alfred's Tower stands on National Trust land near the top of Kingsettle Hill, on the minor road linking the B3081 at Redlynch with the B3092 at Stourton. The tower, which is 160 feet high, is of brick, triangular, with a staircase in one of the angle projections. It was built in 1722 for Henry Hoare of nearby Stourhead, where the eighteenth-century landscapes are considered to be as beautiful as anything of the kind in Europe.

MERE Wiltshire
ST 812322 OS 183
Mere, seven miles east of Wincanton on the A303(T), is revealed from afar by the tower of St Michael's church, which is 124 feet in height. The church incorporates work of all centuries from the eleventh to the twentieth.

EASTLEIGH WOOD Wiltshire
ST 885425 OS 183
Eastleigh Wood is on the north side of a minor road linking Crockerton Green, on the A350 a mile and a half south of Warminster, with Sutton Veney.

EDINGTON Wiltshire
ST 926533 OS 184
Edington is three and a half miles east-north-east of Westbury on the B3098. While no traces of the Anglo-Saxon period have been identified here, the church of St Mary, St Katherine and All Saints, built in the fourteenth century, is described by the architectural historian Pevsner as 'a wonderful church and a highly important church', and is well worth a visit.

WESTBURY Wiltshire
ST 898516 OS 184
The figure of a horse, formed by cutting turf off the underlying chalk, is on a west-facing flank of Westbury Hill, a mile and a half east of All Saints church, Westbury, by the B3098. The horse, which was recut in 1778, is just below the western arc of the perimeter of an Iron Age hillfort, Bratton Castle. As in the case of the well-known hillfort Maiden Castle, near Dorchester, Dorset, there is a Neolithic long barrow of about 3,000 B.C., within Bratton Castle.

the previous two hundred years, and not to be restored again for more than another century, when Alfred's successors fortified it anew before it fell to the forces led by King Cnut. Five miles further to the east the king and his men crossed the little River Cale, where **Wincanton** now stands, and two miles further on he could look northwards to the wooded ridge known as "the high point" (British *pen*) of Selwood – today, **Penselwood**.

And so King Alfred rode to the trysting point, Egbert's Stone, at or near the meeting of the borders of Dorset, Somerset and Wiltshire, some thirty miles from his Athelney base. The precise location of the Stone has not been determined, but the building known as **Alfred's Tower** is said to mark the site. Here the king and the men of Somerset were met by contingents from Wiltshire and from Hampshire west of the River Test. "They rejoiced to see him" writes the compiler of the *Anglo-Saxon Chronicle* with economy of words – and well they might, after months of uncertainty, with but scanty information about the very survival, let alone military effectiveness, of the king. One can imagine the instant burgeoning of morale among the men of various ages and forms of dress and weaponry, as they met around the stone and exchanged news and hopes for the outcomes of their venture.

They settled down for the night in the vicinity of Penselwood. The next day, after prayer and meditation, and such breakfast as they could muster, the whole army moved to the neighbourhood of **Mere**, whence they turned north-east, down the valley then known as Deferreal. This stretch of the upper valley of the River Wylye still preserves a recollection of this name, for its five villages all retain the element Deverill in their titles.

As they began the descent into the valley, the army could look ahead to the north-north-east across to the high ground forming the western extremity of Salisbury Plain, beyond which lay tomorrow's battle-ground. First, however, they were to spend a night in rest and prayer and preparation, for which purpose a place named Iley, only a few miles from the previous night's camp, was selected. This is now in **Eastleigh Wood**, in the crook of the River Wylye.

King Alfred, determined to bring King Guthrum the Viking to battle, may have intended to move towards Chippenham that day for the purpose. But King Guthrum, possibly with a similar idea in mind, had come out of his fortress and was on the march with his army. Just when it was that King Alfred heard of King Guthrum's move is not recorded. But it would appear that he knew when, at dawn, he led his army from Iley, moving for some eight miles over or round the Plain, to **Edington**. Here, on the northern slope of Edington Hill, the royal army won the day. Again, the *Chronicle* understates in masterly manner: "and there fought with all the army, and put them to flight". Achieving this meant a long, hard day for the men of Wessex, culminating in the triumphant moment when they saw the Vikings turn to race for their lives towards their refuge at Chippenham.

It has been supposed that the victory was commemorated by the **Westbury White Horse**, cut in the turf nearby. But it is probable that in fact the horse (which today presents an almost comic caricature of an equine animal) is very much older than that. For the Iron-Age Celts cut images of their tribal gods and cult-animals on the slopes of chalk hills, as witness survivors such as the Oxfordshire Uffington White Horse, the Dorset Cerne

Alfred's Tower

Travellers to Edington are well
advised to visit this grand church of
St Mary, St Katherine and All Saints

An Iron-Age horse with its head in the
clouds over Westbury Hill

The River Avon below Chippenham

Features of St Lawrence's church in
Bradford-on Avon which was already
nearly two hundred years old when
King Alfred came to it in 878

Giant, and the East Sussex Long Man of Wilmington. These hill-figures were, and indeed still are, regularly scoured by people living in their vicinity, often at some calendar festival such as May Day, the work being accompanied by dancing and general merrymaking. It would seem probable, then, that the Westbury White Horse was originally an Iron-Age creation, possibly related to the Celtic hillfort of Bratton Castle above it, from which a breath-taking view extends to the north. Indeed, the old defences may well have been used by one side or the other during the course of the fighting. According to one account, "the horse was 'new-modelled' and altered from 'the cart breed' to 'the blood kind' in 1778, by Lord Abingdon's steward, 'a miserable being of the name of Gee'": and in 1873 it was again "rectified."

King Alfred put the Viking armies to flight with great slaughter and with the taking of many captives, pursuing the survivors right to their stronghold at **Chippenham**. The countryside on the direct route of the chase, thirteen miles as the crow flies, is virtually level, and is only restricted in the area between three and four miles short of Chippenham, where Bowdon Hill rises from quite near to the east bank of the River Avon. On arrival at Chippenham, the more fortunate of the enemy made their way into the stronghold, and shut the gate. Those who failed to get in faced the renewed vigour of the men of Wessex, and many were hewn down after their comrades had barred access to the stronghold. The king then laid siege, and awaited the result, with his triumphant army around him.

The protection afforded to the Vikings by the river on all sides except the south served the English well, for they could easily stop any attempt to get into or out of the defences by water. Likewise, the defensive wall across the neck of the peninsula acted both to keep the Vikings safe, and to allow King Alfred to forbid them any land-borne supplies. The siege was so rigorous that, after only two weeks, the Vikings, starved and brought to low moral and physical condition, sued for peace. They offered to give hostages and take none in return, a thing they had never done before: and to leave Wessex, never to return. Moreover, King Guthrum asked to be received into the Christian faith by King Alfred himself. Thus ended, in triumph for the king and his army, one of the crucial months in England's history. The Battle of Ethandun, as Edington was then called, should ever be remembered.

On his way back the West Country King Alfred had no need to travel again over the route he had covered only two weeks before. He could ride off now to the south-east from Chippenham, up the gentle slope of Derry Hill, and past the then still recognisable ruins of the small Romano-British town *Verlucio*, now **Sandy Lane**, which stood beside the old road between *Cunetio*, Mildenhall, fifteen miles to the east, and *Aquae Sulis*, Bath, thirteen miles to the west. The king could see and perhaps marvel at the ruins – stone columns and blocks, bricks, rubble. For the earlier Saxons, like the Celts, had as a rule used timber for building, and there had been no rush to take stone or brick, as there was to be later when the building of churches and other structures in stone became more the fashion.

From Sandy Lane the king could ride, now unthreatened by ambush and capture, south and west to **Melksham**, to cross the River Avon on the way to **Bradford-on-Avon**. Here King Alfred could worship in the

CHIPPENHAM Wiltshire
ST 920740 OS 173
Chippenham is a market town on the River Avon, six miles north of Melksham on the A350 and A4(T). There is a great deal of interest in the town, from the Norman parts of the church of St Andrew onwards to the present day.

SANDY LANE Wiltshire
ST 965680 OS 173
Sandy Lane is four and a half miles south-east of Chippenham on the A342. Wans House, a small mansion of 1820, is south of the village in a fork between the A342 and a minor road leading off south-east towards Heddington. The site of Verlucio is close to the east side of this minor road. A Romano-British farmstead, or "villa", formerly existed 600 yards north of Verlucio, and another one mile to the south at Bromham.

MELKSHAM Wiltshire
ST 903642 OS 173
Melksham is six miles south of Chippenham on the A350. In the graveyard of St Michael's church there is a yew tree so old that it might have been growing when King Alfred passed after the seige, on his way to Bradford-on-Avon.

BRADFORD-ON-AVON Wiltshire
ST 825610 OS 173
The town is six miles west-south-west of Melksham by the B3107. The seventh-century monastery founded here by St Aldhelm when abbot of Malmesbury is mentioned in a deed of 705, to which date the ground-stage of the existing church of St Lawrence belongs. When King Alfred came in 878, the church was already getting on towards its second centenary. The upper parts of the church as the traveller sees it today were erected in the tenth century; and there are eleventh century modifications. But when we look at the lower levels of the masonry, we are resting our eyes where King Alfred rested his some 1,100 years ago.

BRUTON Somerset
ST 685347 OS 183
Bruton is four miles north of Wincanton by the B3081. It is a small town with a great many remains of the medieval and later periods, among them the magnificent St Mary's church, Sexey's Hospital of 1638, and numerous handsome buildings of the eighteenth and nineteenth centuries.

ALLER Somerset
ST 396288 OS 193
Aller is two miles north-west of Langport on the A372. The church of St Andrew has a thirteenth century doorway in a largely fourteenth century fabric, with a seventeenth century font and pulpit. Among the farm buildings at Aller Court farm are doorways and window-frames of about 1500. Aller is a place which, from early in the Middle Ages, has played an important part in the struggle to drain the Somerset Levels (as the marshlands are known). In 1532 a Court of Sewers was appointed, to improve and direct local sewerage (or drainage) schemes. Over thirty years earlier, in 1499, an officer entitled the Expenditor had been nominated, to disburse the tax money collected for the repair of sewers, or drains. The story of the progress of drainage to the present day is told in the Aller Moor Museum at Burrow Bridge close by.

WEDMORE Somerset
ST 435479 OS 182
Wedmore is eight miles west of Wells on the B3139. The handsome church of St Mary Magdalene has many notable and impressive features, among them a south doorway and other items of about the year 1200, and a magnificent west front. Wookey Hole, a shrine in the Iron Age and Romano-British times, now electrically lit, is six miles to the east along the B3139.

church of St Lawrence, which had been built one hundred and eighty years earlier, and which survives to this day. From Bradford-on-Avon the royal party could ride south, up the valley of the River Frome, skirting the west side of Selwood, to the higher ground at North Brewham, the watershed between the Rivers Frome and Brue. Here the king was only two miles from Egbert's Stone, and once again on familiar ground. But this time he could cut the corner, proceeding to **Bruton** and so south-west, to join the old route just north of Cadbury Castle.

The agreement between Alfred and Guthrum was sealed three weeks later, when the King of the Vikings, with thirty of his companions, came to Alfred at **Aller**. Here, on a low elevation north-east of Aller Moor, there was a royal residence, the site of which is said to be marked today by Aller Court Farm and the adjacent church of St Andrew, the earliest surviving part of which dates from two and a half centuries after the kings' visit in 878. There Alfred stood sponsor to Guthrum at his baptism, and Guthrum put aside his heathen gods. Eight days later the baptism ceremony was completed at **Wedmore**, another royal residence. Guthrum put off the baptismal head-dress, and Alfred bestowed gifts most lavishly on the Viking king and his men.

And so ended the triumphal progress of King Alfred, in the marshlands of Somerset where it had begun, bringing victory to the West Saxons, and setting the country on course for eventual unification. For this great feat King Alfred earned the accolade – ALFRED THE GREAT.

William the Conqueror
The harrying of south-east England
PEVENSEY – WESTMINSTER 1066

Trevor Rowley

William the Conqueror (1027/8–87) was the illegitimate son of Robert, Duke of Normandy (remembered as "Robert the Devil") and Herleva, daughter of William the Tanner, from Falaise. His conviction that he was the rightful heir of the English king Edward the Confessor (d. 1066) was vindicated by his crushing victory over Edward's successor Harold at Hastings in 1066. But the consolidation of William's conquest took years. In the process he largely displaced the Anglo-Saxon aristocracy with a French-speaking one, which was also to infiltrate neighbouring Celtic principalities, a momentous development in the history of the British Isles.

William was tall and well-built; in maturity he was fat and balding. He had a rather hoarse voice and a stern, imposing presence. He was temperate in his habits, conventionally pious and accounted faithful to his wife Matilida, daughter of the count of Flanders. He was a fanatical huntsman. He died at Rouen of internal injuries caused by a fall from a horse and was buried in the abbey of St Étienne which he had founded at Caen. His tomb was destroyed in the sixteenth century.

Remaining memorials to William's power are Battle Abbey, which he founded on the site of the battle of Hastings; his new hunting preserve the New Forest; the White Tower in the Tower of London and the extraordinary land survey, Domesday Book (1086).

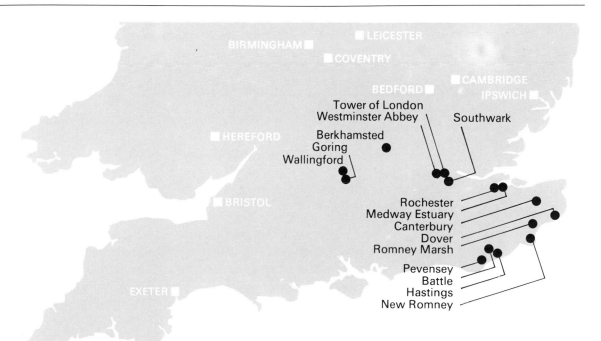

1066 is, as everyone knows, the date when Duke William of Normandy defeated Harold at the Battle of Hastings and thus became king of England. What is not so well known, however, is that after the battle there was a ten week interval before William entered London and was crowned king. In the intervening period William and his victorious army followed a circuitous route through southern England. This journey took the Normans firstly north-eastwards into Kent, then westwards to the Thames at Southwark, then westwards again as far as Wallingford and then north-eastwards along the foot of the Chiltern escarpment to Berkhamsted where the surrender of London was negotiated, then finally into the capital for the coronation ceremony, held on Christmas Day 1066 in Westminster Abbey. Although the main features of the journey are well documented, there is some disagreement amongst scholars over some of the details, particularly the precise dates on which certain events took place.

The chroniclers have provided us with a basic outline of the route taken by the Normans from Hastings to London – but there are gaps and some inconsistencies in the story. Nevertheless many features of William's conquest of England were reminiscent of the Roman conquest of Britain a thousand years earlier, and during this first phase of his occupation it seems highly likely that William utilised the surviving Roman road system wherever possible. Although some sections of Roman road would have fallen out of use, there is enough evidence to show that in south-eastern England at least, the system was still largely intact, and still connecting the principal places that William needed to subdue in order to win the country. According to Florence of Worcester, on his march "Count William was laying waste Sussex, Kent, Hampshire, Surrey, Middlesex and Hertfordshire". It is therefore possible to check the route of this destruction. In the Domesday Book (1086) each manor is normally given three values: pre-1066; "later", i.e. the value at the point where the manor passed to its Norman lord; and "now" (1086). In south-eastern England some land values increased or remained the same immediately after 1066, but there are a significant number whose values decreased, sometimes drastically. The most plausible reason for such a decline is that it is reflecting the damaging effect of the passage of the Norman army. Many manors, particularly around Hastings, are recorded as "laid waste". If we bear in mind that William had several thousand combatants, several thousand horses, and many non-combatants in his army, we have to imagine that the feeding of his host would cause severe problems. Such problems would have been compounded by the nature of the Norman army, which was not a unified professional force but composed of several feudal contingents of varying "nationalities" – Normans, Bretons, Flemings, men from Poitou and Burgundy, and probably even a band from the Norman lands in southern Italy. Food would have to be collected on the way, which in effect would mean the mass seizure of crops and livestock from any farm encountered *en route*. Additionally whenever William encountered opposition he pursued a "scorched earth" policy, pillaging and burning settlements indiscriminately.

Also it should be remembered that the impact of the passage of William's army would have been felt over a far wider area than just the corridor of land traversed by the main body of troops. Considerable damage would have been wrought on adjacent areas, and the longer the army remained in one place the greater the areas which would have suffered.

Duke William's fleet with his army sailed from Saint-Valery in Normandy at nightfall on Wednesday the 27th of September 1066, after having waited there almost three weeks for favourable wind conditions. The Normans landed early the following morning at **Pevensey**, Sussex. This was the Roman *Anderida*, one of the great fortresses of the "Saxon Shore", which in 491 had been taken by raiding Saxons who "slew all that dwelt therein, nor was there one Briton left". Here William rapidly refortified the Roman fort, by digging an inner rampart. Subsequently a Norman castle consisting of a stone keep and a gatehouse was built here in the south-east angle of an enclosure of about ten acres. This enclosure is surrounded by a Roman wall, still standing up to twenty feet high in places and strengthened by a series of round towers.

William needed to maintain close contact with his fleet until a decisive battle had occurred. He therefore moved both his fleet and his army eastwards to **Hastings** which he occupied on September the 29th. Here he could utilise the good harbour facilities. In the eleventh century the configuration of the Sussex coastline was considerably different from today: so that in an emergency the Hastings area could be easily defended while William re-embarked his army. Within the town it is recorded that he erected a fortification, this is almost certainly the one which appears in course of construction on the Bayeux Tapestry – the near-contemporary "strip-cartoon" of the campaign, made in England to the order of William's half-brother Bishop Odo of Bayeux, and still to be seen in the Bishop's Palace there. Also while in Hastings he ravaged the surrounding countryside, and a hint of this appears in the tapestry in the form of soldiers firing a house from which a mother and child are making their escape. Little evidence of these momentous events survives to be seen today. The much eroded promontory castle at Hastings was investigated in the 1960s but failed to provide evidence of the Conqueror's presence. Near the present day pier is a great stone called "the Conqueror's stone" commemorating William's short stay in Hastings, which together with Romney, Hythe, Dover and Sandwich is one of the "Cinque" ports. This confederation of important south-eastern ports was probably founded before William invaded. In exchange for privileges such as self government and tax exemptions, the five towns pledged to supply men and vessels to defend England and her trade. Now the title of "Cinque Port" is an honorary one.

By the middle of October, King Harold of England had marched, with extraordinary speed, the 250 miles from the scene of his victory at Stamford Bridge in Yorkshire (fought on the 25th of September) to the place now known as **Battle**, in memory of the events of the 14th of October 1066, a few miles inland from Hastings. At that time the area was known to the English as "the place of the grey apple tree" and to the Normans it was known as "Senlac" (sandy lake) and it is this imported name which has survived. Senlac hill was the highest rise of ground between Hastings and the present day Battle. It was Harold who chose the site. After the battle of Stamford Bridge he rapidly moved his army southwards and reached the Downs during the night of the 13th/14th of October, apparently taking

PEVENSEY Sussex
TQ 644048 OS 199
The Norman castle at Pevensey, where William landed, sits within Roman fortifications. Built in the third century A.D., it was one of the Saxon Shore forts, and known as Anderida. Though it had probably been abandoned since the massacre of its Romano-British defenders by Saxons in 491, in 1066 William considered its surviving fortifications strong enough to provide the first Norman base on English soil. Later the walls, which stand up to twenty feet high in places, were used as an outer defence for the Norman castle, which was started soon after the Conquest. The inner gatehouse and the inner bailey were added in the thirteenth century; the Old Minthouse which dates from the fourteenth century and lies opposite also deserves a visit.

HASTINGS Sussex
TQ 821094 OS 199
The busy seaside resort and fishing port that has given its name to the battle which changed the course of English history. Although little authentic remains from William's visit there are plenty of mementos of the occasion. Hastings is one of the Cinque Ports and although its harbour has almost disappeared before the encroaching sea the Old Town is well preserved and worth a visit. The so called "Fisherman's church" here is now a fishing museum and the Old Town Hall houses a collection of town history. The ruins of a later medieval stone castle sit on top of William's motte and bailey castle, of which there are few visible remains. Access to the castle is from Castle Hill Road or by lift from George Street. Close to the pier there is a great stone called the Conqueror's stone. The Museum and Art Gallery in Cambridge Road contains an interesting collection of local archaeological and historical material.

BATTLE Sussex
TQ 750159 OS 199
Takes its name from the Battle of Hastings which was fought to the south east of the town-centre. Battle Abbey was founded by William the Conqueror in fulfilment of a vow which he made before the Battle of Hastings. Little remains of the abbey church, but the position of the altar, which was erected on the site where Harold fell, is marked by Harold's stone (a Norman gift of 1903). Norman architecture is visible in the surviving masonry of the abbey. There are good views from the abbey grounds of the heights of Senlac and Telham, which feature in the story of the battle. The famous "Roll of Battle Abbey", a list of Norman participants in the victory, was probably not compiled until the fourteenth century.

A postern in the outer Roman wall of Pevensey Castle

The moat at Pevensey

up his position during the hours of darkness. His troops, however, were clearly in a state of great exhaustion, but were to fight a fateful battle the following day.

When the news of Harold's arrival reached William, he appreciated that he had been given a great opportunity and was quick to seize it. He left Hastings early in the morning of the 14th of October, and when he reached the site of Telham Hill he was aware that Harold was established on the neighbouring summit of Senlac. The armies were evenly matched in numbers, probably with between 5,000 and 7,000 on each side. However, Harold's men followed the English tradition of fighting on foot, whereas William's were largely cavalrymen. During the day William mounted a sequence of unsuccessful attacks on Senlac Hill, but later in the battle he several times employed the favourite Norman tactic of a feigned retreat. Despite the misgivings of Harold and his commanders the Anglo-Saxons chased after the apparently fleeing Normans, who rapidly re-grouped and surrounded the pursuing infantrymen, cutting them to pieces: and finally a group of Normans successfully stormed Senlac Hill, wiping out the remaining English including King Harold and many of the English nobles. These momentous events of the 14th of October are graphically recorded on the Bayeux Tapestry.

William founded a Benedictine abbey on the site of his victory, the high altar of its church reputedly marking the exact spot where Harold and his standard of "the Fighting Man" had fallen. Nothing now remains of that church, but the position of the altar is marked by "Harold's Stone": and, though largely in ruins, the remains of Battle Abbey's other buildings still represent some of the finest examples of Norman architecture in south-east England.

The war, however, was not yet over. William knew that the English could still raise an army to oppose him, and that there were other candidates for the throne still alive; he therefore had to force them to accept him as the only man fit to be king. Additionally William appreciated that even his successful Norman army was incapable of successfully beseiging London, he had to take it by a mixture of intimidation and persuasion. After his victory William returned to Hastings in order to rest his troops for about a week, and to allow time for offers of submission from the surviving English Earls to come in. But no such offers arrived.

According to the chronicler, William of Poitiers, who was a chaplain to the Conqueror, on Friday the 20th of October the Duke "left Hastings in charge of a brave commander, and proceeded to **New Romney**, where he punished at his pleasure those who had previously killed some of his men after a struggle". He apparently sacked New Romney on Friday the 20th of October in reprisal for an attack by the English on some of his foraging troops. By 1066 the port of Old Romney, which during the Saxon period had been a major port on the edge of the ever expanding **Romney Marsh**, had silted up and had been replaced by New Romney. Romney occupied a prime strategic site and was also an important source of naval ships and crews. The problems involved in moving a large force overland to Romney would have been very considerable, requiring either a long inland detour to avoid the many river estuaries in the region, or a series

NEW ROMNEY

TR 065248 OS 189

Old Romney was silted up before the Conquest and New Romney became a major south coast port. There are no obvious remains of William's journey here, but the parish church of St Nicholas was originally an ambitious late-Norman building (whose fine tower still stands) later extended in the fourteenth century. The church, now inland, was built on what was then the seashore. Romney is one of the original Cinque Ports.

ROMNEY MARSH

TR 050300 OS 189

In antiquity Romney Marsh was a dangerous area to cross, with a number of constantly changing tidal estuaries running into the sea here. The coastline, too, has changed considerably over the centuries. It seems likely that William avoided a long inland detour to reach Romney by taking the sea route from Hastings. William's soldiers probably did not penetrate very deeply into the Marsh, although the capture of Romney itself was essential for the success of the campaign.

DOVER Kent
TR 325418 OS 179

Dover has traditionally occupied a strategic site of prime importance and was one of the original Cinque Ports. Dover castle ("the key of England") which overlooks the town and the English Channel was originally a prehistoric fortification which incorporates a rare example of a Roman lighthouse. The present castle dates from the late-Norman period to the nineteenth century. The church of St Mary de Castro within the castle precinct is largely Saxon. The castle complex is approached from Castle Hill Road. St Mary's church in Cannon Street has a remarkable Norman tower. Dover is the starting point of Watling Street which William followed as far as London.

CANTERBURY Kent
TR 152578 OS 179

Canterbury was the Roman town of Durovernum, and was an important commercial port sitting at a major crossroads. It was renamed Cantwaraburg (the fortress of the men of Kent) by the Saxons and after St Augustine's mission here in 597 it became, and remains, the centre of the English church. The oldest portions of the present cathedral were built by Lanfranc, the first Norman archbishop of Canterbury: the "cathedral priory" attached to it (of whose buildings much remains) was the largest Benedictine abbey in Britain. Not far away, and just outside Canterbury's towering city wall, lie the ruins of another great monastery, St Augustine's Abbey. Founded in 598 by Augustine himself, it houses the tombs of many Saxon saints and kings, and was rebuilt by the Normans in 1070: the fascinating excavated remains are open to visit. In the High Street is the Museum which contains an important Roman collection and other local material.

of difficult river crossings. It would seem most probable, therefore, that the attack on Romney was executed by water, either directly from the sea or possibly down the main arm of the River Rother which then reached the sea at New Romney.

The brutality of William's response at Romney appears to have cowed the inhabitants of Dover, who surrendered on the following day. William moved his army to what is now **Dover** castle. Again the easiest route to follow would have been by sea, and it is probable that most of the troops sailed with the naval contingent to Dover harbour, and then met up with the cavalry which had made their way along the coastal Downs through Lympne, Hythe and Folkestone.

At Dover there was a prehistoric earthwork which had been reinforced during the Roman and Anglo-Saxon periods and would have had extensive masonry remains at the time. A Roman lighthouse still survives there. William spent eight days here improving the fortifications. The great stone fortress which now exists, however, is the work of later kings – notably Henry II, John and Henry III: who raised what was arguably the strongest castle in medieval England, with a mighty keep surrounded by a double ring of many-towered walls. Even in the Conqueror's time, nevertheless, the fortifications were formidable enough, for William of Poitiers recalls "this castle is situated on a rock adjoining the sea and is raised up by nature and so strongly fortified that it stands like a straight wall, as high as an arrows flight. Its side is washed by the sea. While its inhabitants were preparing to surrender unconditionally our men (the Normans) greedy for booty set fire to the castle, and the greater part of it was soon enveloped in flames. The Duke, unwilling that those who had offered to surrender should suffer a loss, gave them a recompense in money for the damage to the castle and their property". William of Poitiers goes on to claim that it was at Dover that William and his troops contracted dysentery. From Dover the route to London was straightforward, and William would have followed the line of the Roman Watling Street, which starts at Dover and which is today represented by the A2 trunk road from Dover to Canterbury and Faversham, and thereafter by the A20 or "Old London Road", which runs (to the north of the M2) from Faversham through Sittingbourne to Rochester. From Faversham onwards, therefore, his route lay relatively close to the Thames Estuary: so that the Norman army may have been able to maintain some contact with its ships.

Not far from Dover, William was met by the men of Canterbury, who offered him the city's surrender. **Canterbury** appears to have submitted on Sunday the 29th of October 1066, but it is not clear if William actually spent much time in the city. For some authorities report that he and his men were now so badly affected by dysentery that they were forced to delay for nearly a month at a place called "the Broken Tower". This was near (but not in) Canterbury, and may perhaps have been the abandoned Roman "Saxon Shore" fortress at Richborough near Sandwich: whose thick walls (formidable even now) and sea-coast position may well have offered better security to a weakened force than the close-packed houses of Canterbury. Canterbury, as the headquarters of the English church, was of course a major prize. Its present cathedral, the mother church of England

Top left, the battered profile of the medieval castle which stands high over the town of Hastings, above, the Conqueror's Stone in front of the town's pier. Left, dense sea mists then, as now, prompted the Romans to erect this lighthouse high above Dover harbour

This memorial stone is said to mark the spot where Harold fell in battle

The remains of the abbey founded by Augustine in Canterbury, in 598

Rochester's cathedral predates its castle; both are quite outstanding examples of Norman architecture

A portion of the walling which helps
to protect Rochester Castle's grounds

William's march to Southwark is likely to have taken him by the Medway Estuary, seen here near Stoke

One of the few remaining standing fragments of masonry seen from the motte at Wallingford

ROCHESTER Kent
TQ 743685 OS 178

Watling Street crosses the Medway estuary at Rochester and during the Norman period the city became an ecclesiastical centre second only to Canterbury. The cathedral contains some impressive Norman architecture. The town was also strategically important and the castle, which was begun by Bishop Gundulf, c.1087 (though little of his work remains) represents one of the finest specimens of Norman military architecture in England. The keep (begun c.1127) is 120 feet high and has walls averaging twelve feet in thickness.

SOUTHWARK Greater London
TQ 327804 OS 176

At Southwark William was in sight of his goal, London. However, despite the claims by his biographers that he defeated the English "insurgents" here, he was clearly unable to cross London Bridge and take the capital. At the southern end of London Bridge is Southwark Cathedral. This church of St Saviour and St Mary Overie only became a cathedral in 1905 but within Southwark there are ancient ecclesiastical roots. St Swithun established a college of priests here in the 960's and there was a monastery here at the time of the Conquest. The bishops of Winchester also had their London palace and prison (the famous and original "Clink") close by, but no material traces of these survive, and there are only the merest remains of the first Norman church of St Mary Overie (over the Water). St Mary's and an Augustinian house served by the canons regular of that order dated from the eleventh century, but a disastrous fire of 1206 destroyed virtually everything. It is from the rebuilding after the fire that the ancient parts of the present cathedral date. By the mid fourteenth century a new and fine Gothic church had been constructed: that too was shortly to be severely damaged by another fire, but it was repaired and Southwark was still an important Augustinian house when it was dissolved by Henry VIII in 1539.

THE RIVER THAMES AT STAINES
TQ 033718 OS 176

Willaim's army may have crossed the River Thames at Staines just down stream from Runnymede after travelling westwards along the Roman road from London.

and of Anglicans throughout the world, was begun (on the site of a Saxon predecessor) by William's friend Lanfranc, who replaced the Anglo-Saxon Stigand as Archbishop in 1070: while the magnificent underground crypt is the work of Lanfranc's successor Anselm. But much of what we now see – including the lofty late-Norman choir and the light-filled fourteenth century nave – dates from after 1170, when the cathedral gained new prestige as the shrine of St. Thomas Becket. Elsewhere in the town, St Peter's church has a massive Norman font, and the Norman hall of St Thomas's (Eastbridge) hospital is another notable building. Canterbury castle, which fell into disuse about 1600, was also perhaps begun by William.

About this time William was met by a deputation from Edith, Edward the Confessor's widow, who as Queen-Dowager owned Winchester. Probably following pressure from William, Edith offered him the city of Winchester – an important acquisition, as it housed the royal treasury. Winchester was not included in William's direct route, but it is possible that it was occupied by an army of Norman reinforcements who landed at Southampton and marched due northwards to meet the main body of William's troops. Thus William now controlled much of south-eastern England, but London remained unsubdued. He was therefore determined to isolate the capital. The army eventually marched on by way of **Rochester** and Greenwich and the Duke "established himself not far from London in a place where he knew they met". This place was **Southwark**, a settlement on the other side of the Thames from London. A strong force of English under the control of a contestant for the throne, Edgar the Aetheling (the Confessor's great-nephew), were occupying London; and some of them made a sortie across the river into Southwark; the Norman advance guard drove them back across the bridge, and then burnt "all the buildings on this (the south) side of the river".

Despite the Norman rhetoric which insists that William had "dealt a double blow on the pride of (his) stubborn foes", it seems inconceivable that William would have missed this opportunity of taking London if he had been capable of doing so. The failure to take London at the first attempt represented a serious setback to the Normans, and William may well have felt the need for the help of his reinforcements to quell the city. He therefore moved his main army westwards "without opposition", devastating northern Hampshire and parts of Berkshire. The precise route he took is not recorded. Some scholars contend that he took a southerly sweep to encompass Leatherhead, Guildford, Basing and Wantage. The evidence of destruction in the Domesday Book, however, might suggest a more northerly route along the Thames Valley.

William's most logical route would have been to cross the Thames at Westminster, then proceed westwards down what is now the Kensington Road to join the main Roman road running from London to Staines, where the route again crosses the Thames. From Staines the main body of the army could have continued south-westwards along the Roman road to the now abandoned city of Silchester, or more likely moved directly westwards through Windsor to Reading, which would have been a suitable rendezvous with the Norman reinforcements. The army would then have followed the Thames northwards to Wallingford through the **Goring Gap**, where the river cuts through the Chiltern escarpment. According to the contemporary chronicler William of Jumièges, however, the Conqueror must have followed the south bank of the river, not crossing it at all until he reached Wallingford.

Wallingford is one of the last places actually named in the chronicles on William's circuitous route to London. In the late Anglo-Saxon period Wallingford had been an important fortified town (or *Burh*) and river crossing, and in the Domesday Book (1086) it appears as one of the most important towns in the kingdom. The taking of Wallingford would effectively have sealed off the middle Thames from any uprising. There were already considerable fortifications around the town (they are still clearly visible), but a large motte and bailey castle was erected in the south-eastern quadrant of the Saxon settlement. Thereafter the castle was added to, and in the thirteenth century a new circuit of outer defences appears to have buried part of the early medieval town. Excavations here found cobb (mud) buildings standing to a height of six feet.

At this stage Stigand, the Anglo-Saxon Archbishop of Canterbury, came from London and transferred his allegiance to William. From Wallingford William marched north-eastwards along the ancient line of the Icknield Way which runs along the foot of the Chilterns. The Icknield Way is one of Britain's most important prehistoric trackways, but was used in the Roman period and later. Between Wallingford and Tring the route is duplicated with a Lower and Upper Icknield Way running parallel to each other a mile or so apart. At Tring the ancient trackway meets the Roman Akeman Street, which then follows the Bulbourne valley south-east through the Chilterns, by way of **Berkhamsted**, where the English leaders approached William and offered him the throne. "(William) was met by Archbishop Aldred, and the Aetheling Edgar and Earl Edwin and Earl Morcar, and all the chief men of London, who submitted from force of circumstances, but only when the depredation was complete. It was great folly that they had not done so sooner", continued the gloomy Anglo-Saxon Chronicler, "but God would not remedy matters because of our sins. They gave him hostages and swore oaths of fealty, and he promised to be a gracious liege lord".

Berkhamsted is the final place name recorded in the chronicles, but there is some argument whether the events of 1066 took place in what is now Great Berkhamsted or, rather, at Little Berkhamsted just to the south of Hertford. This alternative itinerary would have taken William on a considerable northerly detour, to encompass such places as Buckingham, Bedford and St Neots: and there is in fact some evidence for this route from the devastation recorded in those areas. Militating in favour of Great Berkhamsted, on the other hand, is the fact that an important castle is sited there, of which some eleventh century Norman work survives. The core of the castle is a motte and bailey, which is an early castle form, and there is a clear relationship between important places in early Norman England and the siting of such castles. William of Poitiers, incidentally, claimed that at the time of the surrender London was in sight, but this would not have been true at either of the Berkhamsteds.

After a short delay William continued towards London, probably along

GORING GAP
SP 601820 OS 175
The River Thames cuts through the Chiltern escarpment at Goring and the Gap here has always been an important historical route between the Upper and Middle Thames valleys. William's army, having been reinforced, may have made their way northwards through the gap to reach Wallingford.

WALLINGFORD Oxfordshire
SU 609895 OS 175
Wallingford was built as a fortified town by King Alfred in order to guard against Viking attacks from the north. Remains of Alfred's fortifications can still be clearly traced within the town. At the time of the Conquest Wallingford was a major river port and commercial centre as well as representing an important strategic prize for William. There are extensive earthworks of the Norman motte and bailey castle, which was started immediately after the Conquest, but only the motte is accessible to the visitor today. There is a small museum in the High Street which traces the town's archaeology and history.

The present bridge is medieval, but there was a bridge here in 1066. The River Thames was navigable as far west as Oxford at this time.

BERKHAMSTED Hertfordshire
SP 995083 OS 165
Great Berkhamsted lies on Akeman Street in the Bulbourne valley, which William's troops were using to cut southwards across the Chiltern escarpment. Berkhamsted Castle is the site normally associated with the final capitulation of the English. The castle remains lie to the north of the town centre (signposted), beyond the Grand Union Canal and railway, and incorporate the earthworks of an early Norman motte and bailey. It remained in Crown hands for much of the Middle Ages and in 1356 King John II of France was imprisoned here after the Battle of Poitiers.

TOWER OF LONDON City of London
TQ 337805 OS 176
The Tower of London, which was started by William within the ramparts of the Roman city walls, was the ultimate architectural statement of the Norman Conquest. It represented the power, dominance and tyranny of the early Norman kings.

WESTMINSTER ABBEY Greater London
TQ 302792 OS 176
William the Conqueror was crowned William I of England in Westminster Abbey on Christmas Day 1066. The building in which the coronation took place had been constructed by Edward the Confessor and consecrated just one year earlier. The present church dates largely from the thirteenth century, but the monastic buildings contain some significant Norman architecture.

Akeman Street as far as St Albans and then across Enfield Chase to join Ermine Street at Enfield. Confusion about the precise route followed is probably compounded by the fact that the army was certainly divided up into a number of contingents by this stage, some of which would have been involved in foraging far and wide – for, in the words of the Anglo-Saxon Chronicle, "they harried everywhere they came". William eventually entered London apparently without much opposition – though one chronicler mentions a skirmish with the citizens near the walls – a few days before Christmas. Arrangements were immediately made for his coronation, which was held in Edward the Confessor's new abbey at **Westminster**. Edward had, in fact, been buried here not twelve months earlier. Ironically the church had preceded William as the first major Norman incursion into Britain, for the Confessor's church – which was totally rebuilt by Henry III in the thirteenth century – appears to to have been based upon the great abbey church at Jumièges on the Seine in Normandy. During the service Norman soldiers outside the abbey misunderstood the shouts which marked the acclamation, and thinking a riot was starting, began to set fire to the neighbouring houses.

Immediately afterwards William began to construct the **Tower of London** in order to control the capital. The Tower was built in the south-east corner of the Roman wall enclosing the city of London. This had been refortified by Alfred in the late ninth century and the Normans also set up here a bastion known as the Wardrobe Tower. Twelve years later, when the Normans had understandably become weary of "the fickleness of the vast and fierce population of London," work began on a great keep to improve the temporary fortifications of 1067. This was the "White Tower" – so called because its masonry was once coated with gleaming whitewash – which still stands complete at the centre of a complex of towered walls, baileys, domestic buildings and outworks added by later kings. Gundulf, the Norman Bishop of Rochester and "a man very competent and skilfull at building in stone", was entrusted with the task: and he raised for William a massive fortified palace complete with great hall and chapel. Roughly a hundred feet square and ninety feet high, its walls (fifteen feet thick at their base) were proof against all known ballistic devices of the time. In its original form it was probably not finished until the end of the eleventh century, so William probably never saw the completed building. Two other major castles were built by the Conqueror in the vicinity of London, Montfichet (near Ludgate) and Baynards Castle (on the Thames near St Paul's Cathedral) but little above-ground evidence for these survives.

After his coronation in **Westminster Abbey**, William moved his army to Barking, thus completing his encirclement of London. While at Barking he summoned a further meeting with English magnates from whom he demanded submission and recognition, and to whom he in return gave a fresh pledge of good government. William had yet to complete his conquest of the country, but he was crowned King of England and in March 1067 felt confident enough to return to Normandy, leaving England in the charge of trusted Norman lords.

The Norman castle motte at Great Berkhamsted, flanked by its attendant moat, banks and ditches

William Rufus
The fatal hunting expedition
GLOUCESTER–WINCHESTER 1100

Anne Ross

William Rufus (c.1060–1100) was a younger son of William the Conqueror and his wife Matilda, a prolific midget. The Conqueror designated his eldest son Robert as duke of Normandy and Rufus as king of England. In 1088 Rufus showed his military and political mettle by suppressing a rebellion of Anglo-Norman barons who preferred Robert's rule. In 1096 Rufus was able to re-unite England and Normandy when Robert, who wished to go on crusade, mortgaged the duchy to him. Rufus was reputed an immensely rich king: he prospered through an efficient and extortionate exploitation of his feudal rights over the aristocracy and Church. His one big mistake, made when he thought he was dying in 1093, was to appoint the saintly Anselm as archbishop of Canterbury. This "feeble old sheep" as Anselm described himself, proved a formidable opponent to the "untamed bull" (the king). Rufus died mysteriously in the New Forest and was buried in Winchester Cathedral.

The nickname "Rufus" was applied to the king by writers of the early twelfth century, because he had a ruddy complexion. He had piercing eyes, stammering speech and a hectoring, jeering manner. He was reputed a daredevil fighter and a generous lord. The darling of the young knights, he never married.

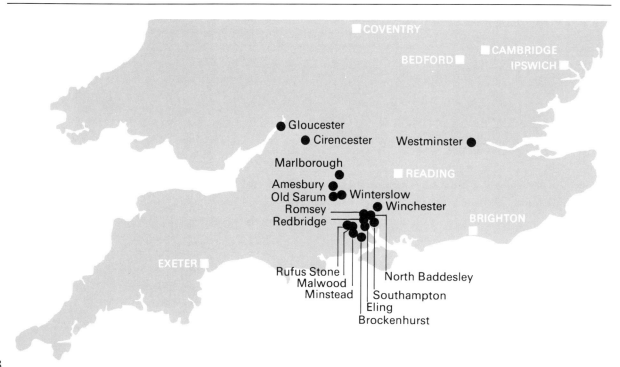

William II, who because of his ruddy complexion, became known as William Rufus – "Le Rus Rei" – "The Red King", was the third son of the first Norman king of England, William I, better known to us as William the Conqueror. He succeeded to the throne of England on the death of his father, and was crowned at Westminster on September the 26th 1087. What kind of man was the much-maligned William the Red, and what were his achievements? Among the many books produced by scholars who have worked on this subject, the most recent, informative and readable is by the eminent historian Professor Barlow, whose work (1983) is cited in the bibliography. The traveller will find full discussion in this of the events surrounding the death of Rufus that are summarised here.

It is difficult for us, from our twentieth century viewpoint, to understand the medieval period, and William Rufus was essentially a man of his time and background. It is much easier to assess his reign, and its place in British history than it is to describe the man.

His chroniclers were men of the Church and in their eyes the king was both an atheist and an extortioner. But although he scorned and ridiculed the Church and exacted from it exorbitant taxes, he was never excommunicated by it, neither was he banned from Christian burial, poor though the ceremony was.

He was essentially a "doer". Positive and quick-thinking; quick to act but not reckless; decisive, imperious and impatient. When roused to anger, which he frequently was, he tended to stammer. William had undeniable faults but many laudable qualities; in an age when the former were rampant, and the latter often little in evidence.

The Church found his undoubtedly worldly court abhorrent. It noted his blasphemous tongue, and resented his lack of respect for its teachings. His courtiers favoured long hair-styles; they liked flamboyant fashions and were regarded as effeminate. Today, however, we can see that William Rufus was first and foremost a soldier; a man of exceptional courage – a warrior king. And if his court resembled a military camp, he was popular with his soldiers, at a time when such popularity was vital to the stability of the country.

Because William never married, and apparently did not indulge greatly in mistresses, he was thought to have homosexual inclinations. This may have been true: but in a soldier-orientated society, it would not have been exceptional; although the Church would have made much of it.

On the death of William the Conqueror, his eldest son Robert became Duke of Normandy by hereditary right, but Rufus, the favourite, received the conquered realm of England by his father's specific will. This division of the Norman lands was the cause of great concern both to William Rufus and his subjects throughout his thirteen year reign. For many Normans held estates in both Normandy and England, and Robert was not lacking supporters who saw him as the rightful King.

In 1088, however, a rising of the barons in Robert's favour was effectively quelled by William, and again in 1095 he suppressed a rebellion led by Robert Mowbray, Earl of Northumberland.

He also pacified the sullen Scots, but Wales presented a more difficult problem. William was ever watchful of the tricky marcher lords of the Welsh

GLOUCESTER Gloucestershire
SO 832185 OS 162

Gloucester, the county town of Gloucestershire, is on the M5. Much of the cathedral (in medieval times St Peter's abbey church) where William Rufus would have worshipped, survives today. The castle, however, which stood beside the River Severn, 400 yards south-west of the cathedral between The Quay and Barbican Road, was demolished in the seventeenth century.

Regional archaeological and natural history collections, and objets d'art, are exhibited in Gloucester City Museum and Art Gallery, Brunswick Road. In Westgate Street, two fifteenth to sixteenth century houses contain relics of local history, crafts, arts and industries, and of the Gloucestershire Regiment.

CIRENCESTER Gloucestershire
SP 025015 OS 163

Cirencester is eighteen miles south-east of Gloucester on the A417(T). The Saxon church in use in Cirencester at the time of William Rufus was soon to be replaced, in 1117, by the Norman structure which preceded the present magnificent largely thirteenth to sixteenth century building. The Norman castle at Cirencester was demolished in 1216. The Corinium Museum, for Cirencester and the Cotswolds, exhibits splendid collections of Roman and Romano-British sculpture and artefacts, and of medieval material. The Tourist Information Centre is on the site of the forum of the Romano-British town, between Dyer Street and Lewis Lane.

MARLBOROUGH Wiltshire
SU 184687 OS 173

Marlborough is ten miles south of Swindon on the A345. William the Conqueror took over a royal estate and borough here, and built a castle of which the motte survives in the grounds of Marlborough College. William Rufus, entering the castle chapel, would have seen the exceptionally large font, of black Tournai marble, which is now in the church of St George, Preshute, a tiny hamlet a quarter of a mile to the west.

AMESBURY Wiltshire
SU 153414 OS 184

Amesbury is five and half miles north of Old Sarum on the A345. Stonehenge is two miles to the west, beside the A344 at 122422.

border and had a hearty dislike of the wild, inclement hinterland of the country. In 1089 he laid claim to Normandy, but it was not until 1096 that Robert, finding his financial problems too much for him, mortgaged the Duchy to William for 100,000 silver marks, which he used to pay for a four-year crusade to the Holy Land.

William Rufus was wilful and ruthless in the pursuit of his own ambitions: which, fortunately for the nation, were to consolidate his English kingdom, free the Duchy of Normandy from the threat of anarchy, and to restore it to its former prosperity. By 1099 he was the acknowledged ruler of both countries and was known as "The Victorious King".

Then, at the height of his power, William Rufus was killed by an errant arrow in the sunlit silence of the New Forest – where a tragic accident had befallen his older brother, Richard, some thirty years earlier. Shortly before his death, Eadmer, the Canterbury monk, was to write of William: "In war and in the acquisition of territory he enjoyed such success that you would think the whole world smiling upon him".

In 1099 William Rufus, following his father's custom, held his Christmas Court and "crown wearing" at **Gloucester** – an important centre of the early Norman kings. William the Conqueror had summoned his Council here in 1085, at St Peter's Abbey, to undertake the planning and making of the Domesday Book. It was here too that William Rufus had been nursed back to health from a near fatal illness in 1093. From Gloucester he could cast a wary eye over Wales and, in the nearby Forest of Dean, indulge in his favourite sport of hunting.

Some time after the Christmas observances and celebrations, he left Gloucester, and travelling by way of **Cirencester**, **Marlborough** and **Amesbury**, he arrived at the windy hilltop town now called **Old Sarum**. In late prehistoric times, the great earthworks there formed the defences of a town of the British tribe, the Celtic Dobunni. After many changes of name, it had by the time of the Domesday Book in 1086 become known as "Sarisberie".

When the See called Sarum became independent in the 1070's, the Bishop, St Osmund, built a cathedral in the north-west sector of the great enclosure. It was consecrated in 1092, and at that time Osmund had already made progress with the building of a castle at the centre of the enclosure on a spacious, flat-topped mound. At the time of the visit of William Rufus, the castle was undoubtedly still of timber construction.

William remained at Old Sarum until Easter, which fell that year on April the 1st. During his time there he engaged in hunting at nearby Clarendon, while attending to the future of the Sarum bishopric which had been vacated by the death of Osmund early in the previous December.

He then travelled by way of **Winterslow** and across the Test Valley, in order to celebrate Easter Day – as was the custom – at the old English capital of **Winchester**. This was the principal repository of his treasury. Formerly housed in the palace, it was moved to the castle before 1100, the old residence having been gradually run down in favour of a new one in the castle. 1093 had seen the first consecration of the new Norman cathedral; and the Saxon Old Minster was pulled down in the same year, Norman taste and liturgical practice having rendered it unsuitable, although

OLD SARUM Wiltshire
SU 138327 OS 184

There is a free carpark within the precincts of Old Sarum, reached by an access road leading west off the A345, just north of the crest of the hill near the Castle Hotel. The great mound, or motte, of the early Norman castle, together with its encircling ditch, survive today in the middle of the enclosure. All traces of St Osmund's castle have long been obliterated by the now-ruinous stone-built constructions which were erected from time to time over the next three hundred years. But the old Celtic outer defences still survive, after some fifteen hundred years of active service. The foundations of St Osmund's cathedral, and those of its successor, can still be seen, beautifully laid out. Looking south from the ramparts down to the low ridge between the Rivers Avon and Bourne, Rufus would have seen a village with a church. Early in the thirteenth century, the cathedral and town on the hill were abandoned, and a new cathedral and town, Salisbury, were established in the area between the rivers. The old village church, St Martin's, much altered since Norman times, is now engulfed in the city. Besides St Martin's, the traveller should see the magnificent cathedral, and visit the Salisbury and South Wiltshire Museum in the beautiful Close. Collections illustrating the natural and social history of Salisbury and neighbouring parts of Wiltshire include fascinating and informative models of Old Sarum and Stonehenge. There are numerous carparks, including a tower, within a quarter of a mile of the Close.

WINTERSLOW Wiltshire
SU 229325 OS 184

Four miles north east of Salisbury leave the A30 by the secondary road to the right, to Winterslow. The church of All Saints has early Norman features in the south arcade, which formed part of the church standing here when William Rufus passed on his way to Winchester.

Rufus worshipped in Gloucester's Benedictine abbey church, which was not raised to cathedral status until 1541

WINCHESTER Hampshire
SU 478295 OS 185

Winchester, the county town of Hampshire, is on the M3. In the first century AD the Roman government in Britain formed a territory, Civitas Belgarum, in the region extending from Winchester on the east to Bath on the west, from the Solent on the south to Salisbury Plain on the north. The administrative centre was Venta Belgarum, a new town built on the east-facing flank of the valley of the river Itchen. The town became Wintanceaster, capital of Wessex and, from the ninth to the eleventh centuries, capital of England. William the Conqueror built a palace immediately north-west of the cathedral, and a motte and bailey castle, now the site of the Great Hall where the Round Table is exhibited. William Rufus would have seen the castle, the palace and the newly rebuilt cathedral, finished in 1098, much of which survives in the present magnificent structure.

WESTMINSTER London
TQ 302795 OS 176

The Palace of Westminster, now the Houses of Parliament, is on the left bank of the River Thames in London, near Westminster Bridge. Public carparks in the vicinity are small and few, and the traveller is advised to make other arrangements.

The principal residence of the Norman kings in London was not the Tower but Westminster Palace, on an island formed by the River Thames, the Tyburn and an unnamed stream. William Rufus greatly extended the palace begun by King Edward the Confessor (reigned 1042 to 1066) Westminster Hall, the only part of that palace to survive, was its main feature, a magnificent structure 240 feet in length within walls some seven feet thick.

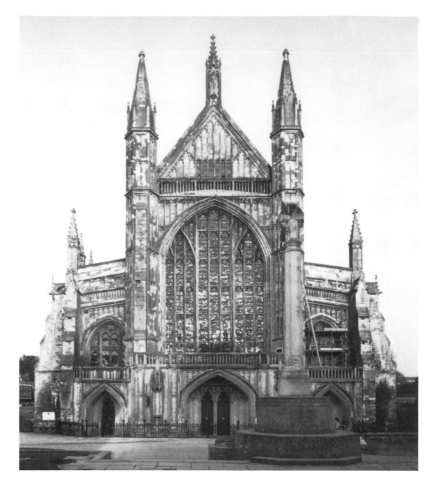

Top, Winchester Cathedral, and below, the retired bridges which still span the River Test at Redbridge

the site remained hallowed.

After observing Easter at Winchester, the King journeyed to **Westminster** and held his Whitsun court there. During that May month, a singular and seemingly portentous incident took place in the New Forest, where William's brother Richard had been killed some thirty years previously. For the King's nephew, another Richard, was mortally wounded while hunting deer, by an arrow fired by one of the company. The courtier immediately took flight and sought refuge in the Cluniac Priory of Lewes. This tragedy did not however dissuade William from his hunting, which was to end with equal drama.

During the summer of 1100, the King left Westminster and travelled to his hunting lodge at, or near **Brockenhurst** in the New Forest. How he made the journey is not certain. He may have come to **Southampton** by sea, and entered the New Forest by crossing the river Test at **Redbridge**. This area seems to have served as a provisioning base for the Crown. Nearby, one of the oldest churches in the New Forest is St Mary's in the village of **Eling**, tucked away among the tidal mudflats at the head of Southampton Water.

Appearing in the Domesday Book as "Edlinges", the parish contained a number of manors. Cola, a forest huntsman, was a sub-tenant of Langley in William's day, and his brother held land at Marchwood, all rented from Edward the Confessor. About 1050, Eling Manor was bound, as part of the manorial dues to the Crown, to find half a day's entertainment for the King while visiting. William the Conqueror retained Eling in his own hands, and the church at that time underwent extensive repairs as can still be seen by the eleventh century Norman workmanship, and the style of the chancel and nave.

After the Conquest, the parish was divided up into a number of manors, including Rumbridge and Testwood. The manor of Rumbridge was granted to Cobb the Smith, for a rent of fifty to a hundred arrows, to be paid to the king when he should enter the New Forest by way of Redbridge.

There is good reason to believe that the arrow which was to kill William Rufus, was made by a member of the Cobb family.

It would seem likely, therefore, that William Rufus, on his way to Brockenhurst, stopped at Eling for hospitality, and in order to collect his rent in arrows and other commodities.

William the Conqueror had declared the New Forest, his favourite hunting ground, to be a royal preserve, subject to strict laws governing rights of access and the taking of game. To improve its hunting amenities some houses and villages were destroyed, and this, together with the prompt and pitiless penalties which swiftly followed any infringements of the new laws, provoked much hostility.

It has been suggested that formerly the New Forest extended from North Baddesley to South Baddesley, names which contain the Saxon words "Badda", a personal name, and "Leah", meaning woodland; and that the forest had been known as "Badda's Leah". Apart from the place names, however, there is no record of this; and no element of the old name survived in the title "Nova Foresta" which appears in the Domesday Book.

BROCKENHURST Hampshire
SU 304017 OS 196
The map reference is to the church of St Nicholas, Brockenhurst, four miles south of Lyndhurst by the A337 and a secondary road, just outside a gate of Brockenhurst Park. Stonework of the Saxon and Norman periods survives in the fabric of the church.

SOUTHAMPTON Hampshire
SU 420120 OS 196
Southampton, on the M27, is twelve miles south of Winchester on the A33. Towards the end of the eleventh century Southampton, then Hamton, was rectangular in shape, bounded to south and west by the water frontage, and to east and north by palisades. The north-south axis was formed by English Street, now High Street, to the west of which was the French quarter in which St Michael's church was built. William Rufus would have seen this and, amongst other buildings, the church of the Holy Rood. Most other structures were of timber. There were landing stages on the west and south of the town.

God's House Tower museum, Town Quay is an early fifteenth century fortification now an archaeology museum. Other museums are the Bargate Guildhall Museum, High Street; Tudor House Museum, St Michael's Square; and the Maritime Museum, Bugle Street, a fourteenth-century wool store now a museum of shipping.

REDBRIDGE Hampshire
SU 368138 OS 196
The old, now disused, bridges over the River Test are accessible from the eastbound carriageway of the A36 immediately before this too crosses the river.

ELING Hampshire
SU 367124 OS 196
Eling lies on either side of the Bartley Water where this joins Southampton Water. The village is reached by turning off either carriageway of the here elevated A35 as this by-passes Totton.

This short stretch of the Roman wall, which contained the town of Corinium, may be seen in Cirencester's Abbey Gardens

Trees need to maintain a tenacious grip on the exposed summits of Old Sarum's Celtic ramparts

All Saints church, Winterslow

All Saints church, Minstead, and
below, a Celtic-inspired memorial in
the churchyard of St John's, North
Baddesley

William Rufus's tomb in the presbytery of Winchester Cathedral
Reproduced by courtesy of the Dean and Chapter of Winchester Cathedral

MALWOOD CASTLE Hampshire
SU 277121 OS 195
"Malwood Castle" ("Fort" on the map), nearly one mile north of Minstead church on a minor road, is an earthwork of unascertained date, in which a private house, "Malwood" (1883) now stands.

MINSTEAD Hampshire
SU 281108 OS 195
Minstead is two and a quarter miles north-north-west of Lyndhurst by the A337 and a secondary road. It is said that stones from a demolished building at Malwood were incorporated in the walls of All Saints church.

RUFUS STONE Hampshire
SU 269125 OS 195
The Rufus Stone stands at the west side of a forest road which winds south for a mile and a half between Brook village, a mile and a half west of Cadnam on the B3079, to a point on the eastbound carriageway of the A31(T) a mile and three quarters south-west of Cadnam. The Stone is encased within a three-sided cast iron pylon, on which is the following inscription in high relief

"Here stood the Oak Tree on which an arrow shot by Sir Walter Tyrrell at a stag glanced and struck King William the second surnamed Rufus on the breast, of which he instantly died, on the second day of August anno 1100.

King William the second, surnamed Rufus being slain, as before related, was laid in a cart, belonging to one Purkis, and drawn from hence, to Winchester, and buried in the Cathedral Church, of that City.

That the spot where an Event so Memorable might not hereafter be forgotten; the enclosed stone was set up by John Lord Delaware, who had seen the Tree growing in this place.

This stone having been much mutilated, and the inscriptions on each of its three sides defaced, this more Durable Memorial, with the original inscriptions, was erected in the year 1841, by Wm Sturges Bourne, Warden."

At the time of his death, the King was based at his hunting lodge at Brockenhurst, but according to tradition, he spent the night of August the 1st at **Malwood Castle**, near **Minstead**.

From that night, the scene for the ensuing drama was set. There were many portents of the death of the King before the event. These are carefully noted by the chroniclers and William Rufus would seem to have had some forewarning.

On August 1st – Lammastide, the feast of St Peter's Chains and the beginning of the "fat season" for deer – the king should have been hunting. The fact that he was not is of some importance to the story.

He seemingly became ill and an attempt may have been made on his life by poison. Other chroniclers, however, suggest that he had a hangover: and others again tell how during the night, he had woken up the household with a great cry and told of a terrible dream he had experienced, warning of his own death, and of much blood.

The following morning, at any rate, he stayed long in bed because of his indisposition, and while there, a monk from Gloucester came to him, on the point of exhaustion, and told him of a dreadful dream which he himself had dreamt, concerning the King's approaching death as a punishment for oppressing the Church. William, however, scorned this ecclesiastical warning, and late in the afternoon went to the hunt.

He was accompanied by his younger brother Henry, and by a group of friends (including Walter Tirel, Lord of Poix) and some foresters.

According to one chronicle William was standing under an oak tree, sheltering his eyes from the sun in the clearing, when the fatal arrow, fired allegedly at a deer, struck him on the breast, whereupon he fell forward to the ground, and died instantly.

The exact spot in the forest where the body is alleged to have fallen, originally shadowed by an ancient oak tree, is now marked by a stone. Local signposts marked "**Rufus Stone**" guide many curious sightseers to the spot visited by Charles II, and indicated by a stone (now encased in cast iron) which tells the legend, in simple words, of the killing of the King of England.

At this horrifying event, the King's companions panicked. Because he had apparently been alone with the King at this time the blame fell on Walter Tirel, who claimed consistently thereafter (even on his death bed), that he was innocent of any murderous intent. To avoid hasty vengeance, however, he rode to the coast and took ship for France.

Henry and the others made immediately for Winchester, where they seized the treasury. They then rode at all speed to London, and on August the 4th, Henry was declared King of England.

The King's body was left unattended, and according to legend was found in the evening by a forest man named Purkis. At some stage, the dead king seems to have been robbed of his hunting clothes, and his body left covered with a ragged cloak.

Purkis took the body in his cart, under cover of darkness, to Winchester. The route was by way of **Romsey**, and according to tradition, **North Baddesley**. Here it was rested at a place then known as Body Farm. Every year on the anniversary of the King's death, the roads traversed by the charcoal burner are still said to run with blood – in memory of the time when Rufus's body "bled like a wild boar pierced with spears" all the way to Winchester.

There are several accounts of the royal burial:

Some, basically, state that the corpse was received by the clergy in the presence of a fitting number of magnates, early on the morning of August the 3rd. Ceremony, however, was scant, no church bells were rung, no alms were distributed to the poor. A tomb was opened in the cathedral, and William was buried under the tower, which collapsed some years later, in 1107, giving rise to much superstitious speculation. Other and less reliable accounts, however, hold that the body was interred in secret and at the dead of night.

On August the 27th 1868, William Rufus's tomb in Winchester Cathedral was opened, preparatory to its removal to its present position in the presbytery, immediately east of the choir. The skeleton was subjected to forensic analysis and was shown to be that of a man of middle height and in full vigour, and this accords well with contemporary descriptions of him. The strange death of William Rufus is still debated hotly by forest folk.

Some sources believe that the Church was ultimately responsible for despatching the anti-Christian King. But others hold that the murder was the responsibility of William's brother Henry, who was certainly present, and who undoubtedly had the best motive for encompassing the King's death – which he lost no time in profitting by. If this is so, however, it is perhaps strange that he subsequently neither rewarded Tirel nor had him put out of the way: and it may well be that Henry (the hardest-headed and most devious of the Conqueror's sons) simply took advantage of a genuine hunting accident.

There is yet another theory which may have more than a little truth in it. The king may have been the victim of a ritual killing, carried out by the people of the forest, who adhered to their ancient pagan beliefs, and hated the son of the man who had imposed his stern laws on their land.

The Anglo-Saxon Chronicle, nevertheless, comments only briefly on the shocking accident: "On the morning after Lammas King William was shot by an arrow by one of his own men".

Whatever William Rufus may have achieved in life, is today overshadowed by the manner of his death.

ROMSEY Hampshire
SU 351211 OS 185
Romsey is ten miles south-west of Winchester by the A3090 and A31. The nunnery in Romsey, founded in 907, flourished in the lifetime of William Rufus. The original church, which the king could have visited, was reconstructed in the twelfth century, and much of this magnificent building still survives. Romsey Town Hall (1866) is situated on the corner of Bell Street and The Square. Beside the side door, in Bell Street, over which is engraved COUNTY COURT, *is an iron plate with a raised inscription reading*

BELL STREET
BODY OF KING WILLIAM RUFUS
CARRIED THROUGH HERE
ON WAY TO
WINCHESTER FOR BURIAL

NORTH BADDESLEY Hampshire
SU 402208 OS 185
St John's church and Body Farm (now renamed Fairfields Farm) are situated three quarters of a mile north-east of the traffic lights in the village at the junction of Nutburn Road and the A27, two and a half miles east of Romsey.

The Rufus Stone

King Stephen
The Thames Valley campaign
WAREHAM–OXFORD 1142

Anthony Goodman

Stephen (*c*.1096–1154) was born a Frenchman, the third son of Stephen count of Blois and Chartres and of Adela, daughter of William the Conqueror. Before 1125 his uncle Henry I of England gave him as a bride Matilda (d. 1152), heiress to the county of Boulogne. On Henry's death in 1135, Stephen seized the English throne. Successful as a count, he was disastrous as a king. He mishandled the English Church and the Anglo-Norman baronage, enabling Henry I's only surviving child and designated heir, Matilda, to establish herself in England as a rival claimant to the throne. The disruption caused mainly by the interminable civil wars between Stephen and Matilda has earned the period a bleak label – "the Anarchy". Stephen's one melancholy distinction as a king is that he fought more often to stay one than any other king of England from the Norman Conquest onwards. The death of his elder son Eustace in 1153 facilitated the end of civil war, by his recognition of Matilda's son Henry as his successor. Stephen died at St Martin's Priory, Dover, leaving a son, William (d. 1159) and a daughter, Mary (d. 1182), who were both to inherit the county of Boulogne. Henry II succeeded Stephen peacefully as king.

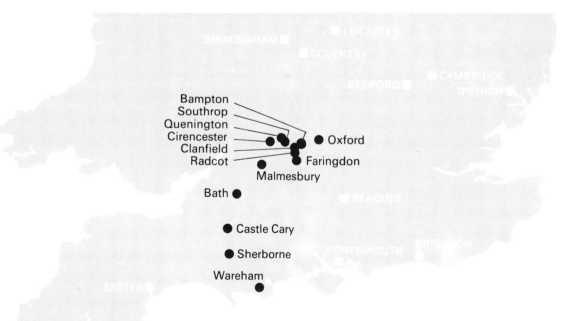

Stephen was probably born about the year 1096. A younger son, he was named after his French father, the count of Blois and Chartres – an unimpressive if genial personality compared to Stephen's formidable mother Adela, daughter of William the Conqueror. By 1113 Stephen was being educated at the court of his uncle Henry I of England (the Conqueror's youngest son). The boy became Henry's favourite nephew and was built up by him as a principal magnate. In 1126 Stephen was one of the notables whom Henry induced to swear allegiance to his daughter Matilda as his successor. But when Henry died in 1135, Stephen quickly seized the English throne. The Anglo-Norman aristocracy (who disliked both the idea of a female ruler and Matilda herself) regarded him as a suitable king and duke of Normandy and he soon received their general recognition. But in the next few years his political mistakes enabled Matilda to win support for her claim, which she promoted by landing in England in 1139. The mainstay of her cause was her half-brother, the illegitimate Robert Earl of Gloucester, whose character and ability better fitted him to rule than either his irascible sister or the genial Stephen.

In 1141 Earl Robert captured Stephen at the battle of Lincoln, but was himself captured by Stephen's supporters at Winchester later that year. The two prisoners were soon exchanged, but the civil war continued until 1153, when it was ended by Stephen's recognition that Matilda's son Henry should succeed him. Stephen fell suddenly and violently ill the following year of what appears to have been a thrombosis resulting from haemorrhoids, which may have resulted from hard living on campaign.

We do not know what Stephen looked like. There is no contemporary description of him and his tomb in the abbey which he founded at Faversham (Kent) has disappeared. He had a soft or weak voice, but great stamina. Unlike many leading nobles, he managed to combine virtues admired by both clerics and laymen. As a young man he conspicuously eschewed fashionable drunkenness and lasciviousness. Despite this, he was regarded as a good knight. He was certainly physically courageous. At the battle of Lincoln he defended himself in turn with a double-headed axe and a sword until they broke, and was captured only when felled by a stone. His biographer described him as exceptionally unassuming, generous and courteous, but was troubled by his inability to distinguish good from bad advice. Remarkably, William of Malmesbury, in a history written to please Stephen's arch-enemy Robert of Gloucester, says that Stephen, when he was a count, "had by his good nature and the way he jested, sat and ate in the company of even the humblest, earned an affection that can hardly be imagined": and that he was "a very kindly man, who, if he had acquired the kingdom in a lawful way and in administering it had not lent trusting ears to the whispers of the ill-disposed, would certainly have lacked little that adorns the royal character".

The best pen-portrait of Stephen is to be found in an unlikely source, a thirteenth-century life of William Marshal, Earl of Pembroke. The information about Stephen in it is doubtless derived from the aged William's reminiscences of his childhood. When William was five or six, he was given by his father John FitzGilbert as a hostage to Stephen for the observance of a truce during the latter's siege of Newbury Castle in Berkshire (1152).

But FitzGilbert broke the truce, and Stephen's entourage urged him to hang the boy. When FitzGilbert refused to save his son by surrendering the castle, therefore, Stephen ordered his men to lead William to a tree. The boy asked the earl of Arundel, who was twirling a javelin, if he could have it. In face of the boy's innocence, Stephen's resolution faltered: taking him in his arms, he carried him back to camp. Subsequently his men suggested that William be hurled into the castle from a siege engine, but again Stephen refused, and he kept the boy for two months with his army before Newbury. One day during that time the king was sitting in a tent strewn with varicoloured flowers, where William wandered about picking plantains. When he had gathered enough, he asked the king to play "knights" with him: this involved trying to strike off with your own bunch the heads of your opponent's. Stephen readily agreed to play and William gave him a bunch, asking him to decide who should strike the first blow. Stephen told William to do so, and the child promptly struck off the head of the king's "knight". The boy was very pleased with his victory and loudly greeted a servant whom his mother had sent to see how he was, who peeped into the tent and swiftly made off before the king's men could catch him.

This account reveals an unexpectedly delightful side of Stephen. Indeed, he had darker sides: when king he could act as a treacherous lord and cruel enemy. But after years of dealing with opponents whom his biographer likened to "the fabled hydra of Hercules" – whose heads grew again as soon as they were cut off – the ageing Stephen (presumably by then a chronic sufferer from haemorrhoids) refused to vent his troubles on a child. He lacked the requisite degree of ruthlessness which made William the Conqueror and his sons Rufus and Henry I successful but hated rulers.

When King Stephen celebrated Christmas at Canterbury in 1141, he had just endured the most unquiet of the six unquiet years of his reign. In the cathedral on Christmas Day he had himself crowned for a second time by the archbishop, in order to remove the stain of his recent captivity. In April 1142 Stephen was in York, re-asserting his rule in the north. Determined to deal decisively with Matilda, he marched south assembling troops, but he fell ill at Northampton and did not recover till June. He had to dismiss many of his soldiers. It looked as if he had missed the opportunity that campaigning season to cripple Matilda, whose cause had been weakened by the defeat at Winchester in 1141. Her principal southern regions of support, centring on Bristol and Gloucester, remained reasonably intact. Her adherents occupied strongholds in the Thames valley as far east as the Oxford region, vitally threatening Stephen's grip on the eastern parts of the realm and his communications northwards. The respective noble partisans of either side dug themselves in at the towns and villages which they had inherited, been granted or had seized, strengthening the ditches and ramparts of boroughs and castles or hastily erecting new fortifications of earth and wood. Within them they stationed small groups of knights, together with horses, attendants and foot soldiers. These guarded and lived off the resources of the neighbouring communities. Each summer campaigning season, the fortunes of the royal protagonists turned on their ability to assemble a superior force mainly from such garrisons (particularly several hundred knights) and hold them long enough in the field with inducements of pay, victuals and plunder, without coincidentally weakening control in the areas they held.

Whilst Stephen lay sick at Northampton, Matilda was planning political moves in the formidable fortress at Devizes (Wiltshire). There she probably said farewell to Earl Robert, who sailed from Wareham (Dorset) after the 24th of June for Normandy, in order to get help from her husband Geoffrey Count of Anjou. Matilda went to Oxford with a strong force, possibly in anticipation of an attack on it by Stephen from the Northampton or London area. She probably stayed in the residence, Beaumont Palace, built by her father Henry I outside the North Gate of the city (at the west end of the present Beaumont Street). Stephen recognised Robert's removal to Normandy and Matilda's to Oxford as a splendid opportunity for him to take the offensive, which he was now well enough to exploit. He did the unexpected. Instead of attacking Oxford, before the end of June he appeared before **Wareham**. The town, lying between the Piddle and Frome rivers, still retains its early rectangular plan and its enclosure on three sides by earthen ramparts. It was probably designed in this form for King Alfred in the ninth century, to safeguard against attacks by the Danes. The stone walls added to the ramparts in the late tenth or early eleventh century have disappeared, but the western rampart (West Walls) was still considered strong enough to be worth strengthening against tank attack in 1940. There was a Norman castle in the south-west angle of the town defences. On the site a modern house (Castle Close) stands on a flat-topped mound overlooking the Frome. Excavations have revealed the foundations of a massive keep within the mound, which may have been built in the early twelfth century. But in 1142 Matilda's garrison was small and probably disconcerted by Stephen's sudden appearance. He easily gained entrance to the town, burnt and plundered it and seized the castle. He left a picked body of knights to guard Wareham and probably secured other strongpoints on the Dorset coast in order to impede Earl Robert's return. Then Stephen again did the unexpected. Instead of now moving directly on Oxford, he apparently went northwards, eventually riding into Cirencester, the centre of a network of Roman roads in a triangle between Matilda's bases at Bristol, Gloucester and Oxford.

Professor Ralph Davis has surmised that he went from Wareham to Cirencester by way of Sherborne, **Castle Cary**, Bath and Malmesbury, which were held by his supporters, who may have provided him with supplies and reinforcements. The strength of the "Old Castle" which his men held at **Sherborne** is still apparent. Raised between 1107 and 1135 by that mighty builder Roger Bishop of Salisbury, the ruins strikingly illustrate William of Malmesbury's remark that there (as at Devizes) "he had raised masses of masonry, surmounted by towers, building over a great extent of ground". Bishop Roger, as royal justiciar, had been head of Henry I's administration: his sophisticated love of luxury is reflected at Sherborne in the grouping of ranges of buildings, including the keep, around a courtyard, probably then a novel arrangement in England. In 1139 Stephen had arrested the bishop and his leading kinsmen and seized their castles. At **Bath** Stephen also held a strong position, well garrisoned. Several years

WAREHAM Dorset
SY 925873 OS 195
Wareham is at the head of the Frome estuary, six miles west of Poole.

An important Anglo-Saxon "burh" or fortified town, it is still largely confined within its Alfredian ramparts, and laid out in its original grid pattern. St Mary's church, founded c.600 by St Aldhelm, was one of the largest Saxon "minsters" of the region, but was much restored in Victorian times. St Martin's also contains Saxon features, and the tomb of T. E. Lawrence ("Lawrence of Arabia").

CASTLE CARY Somerset
ST 643323 OS 183
Castle Cary is three miles south-west of Bruton. Earthworks remain of the castle garrisoned for Stephen, on a hill north-east of the church, and the outline of its large square keep is marked out on the ground.

SHERBORNE Dorset
ST 640165 OS 183
Sherborne is five miles east of Yeovil. Minor Saxon features can be seen in Sherborne Abbey (once a cathedral, the seat of Alfred's biographer Bishop Asser) and parts of the major rebuilding begun in the early twelfth century by Bishop Roger of Salisbury: but most of the present magnificent church is of the fifteenth century, with some splendid fan-vaulting. The extensive remains of Bishop Roger's "Old Castle", much battered during the Civil War siege, include a great gatehouse: and nearby is the "New Castle", an Elizabethan and Jacobean mansion begun by the famous Sir Walter Raleigh and continued by the Digby family, who still own it.

BATH Avon
ST 751647 OS 172
Bath is twelve miles south-east of Bristol. Though now best known for its magnificent Georgian terraces and squares, this famous spa also possesses a virtually complete Roman bath-house system, the best preserved Roman monument in Britain. Its most notable medieval building is Bath Abbey (nominally a cathedral) largely rebuilt after 1499 by Bishop King, secretary to Henry VII: the west front displays carved Tudor badges and the bishop's device of angels and ladders, a reference to the dream which prompted the rebuilding. Nothing remains of the castle.

before he had personally inspected the town defences and ordered the walls to be strengthened. If he went there in 1142, he may have taken the waters, a comfort after his recent illness: for Bath was famous as a spa even then. His biographer described how: ". . . little springs through hidden conduits send up waters heated without human skill or ingenuity from deep in the bowels of the earth to a basin vaulted over with noble arches, creating in the middle of the town baths of agreeable warmth, wholesome and pleasant to look upon . . . the sick are wont to gather there from all England to wash away their infirmities in the health-giving waters, and the whole to see the wondrous jets of hot water and bathe in them."

Compared to the fortifications at Sherborne and Bath, those occupied by Stephen's men at **Malmesbury** are likely to have been flimsy. William of Malmesbury says that Bishop Roger of Salisbury began building a castle there "actually in the churchyard, hardly a stone's throw from the abbey". This sacrilegious excrescence has completely disappeared, but much of the impressive twelfth-century abbey church remains, though it is not clear whether it had been substantially rebuilt when the monk William and Stephen's soldiers were living uneasily cheek by jowl there in 1142.

At **Cirencester** the castle was also a cuckoo in the monastic nest. Matilda's supporters had thrown it up next to the church of the new abbey of Augustinian canons endowed by her father, a juxtaposition which jarred on contemporary religious sensibilities. This castle, wrote a cleric disapprovingly, was "like another Dagon by the Ark of the Lord". When Stephen arrived, it was deserted. He had it fired and its stockade and ramparts thoroughly demolished. Then the royal army swung eastwards along a line of communications between Matilda's western bases and Oxford. Probably, for the sake of speed, it went some way along a Roman road, Akeman Street, and it may have passed near or through the villages of Quenington and Southrop. Their parish churches have remaining features which reflect the growing prosperity of the wool-rich Cotswolds and the receptivity of society to reforming religious precept, trends which the civil war had failed to reverse. In the tympanum over the north door of **Quenington** church is a twelfth-century sculpture of the Harrowing of Hell, a reassurance that, though it might seem in a time of oppressions that, as the Anglo-Saxon Chronicle put it, "Christ and His saints slept", the scriptures gave hope. On the twelfth-century font in **Southrop** church, Moses is sculpted with the Tablets, flanked by figures representing the Church, with chalice and pennoned cross, and the Jewish Synagogue, blinded and with a broken staff – Antisemitism was a concomitant of contemporary religious fervour. So was crusading: a few years after Stephen's 1142 campaign, many of those who had fought in the civil wars were to seek remission of their sins on the Second Crusade. The kind of arms and armour borne by those who campaigned in the Cotswolds in 1142, and those who were to reach the Holy Land, are to be seen in the figures of Virtues trampling Vices on the font.

Stephen's men proceeded to attack garrisons west of Oxford. At **Bampton** they stormed the church tower, on top of which Matilda's garrison had erected a fortification. The Saxon origin and impressive workmanship of this tower were commented on by a contemporary chronicler: parts

The Anglo-Saxon embankment which once protected the population of Wareham against would-be invaders, is today an attractive public amenity

The church of St Martin marks the site of the north gate into ancient Wareham

The ruins of Bishop Roger of Salisbury's great castle at Sherborne

The south front of Malmesbury Abbey

The Abbey's magnificent Norman porch

The remains of Malmesbury Abbey's once tall tower

The twelfth century sculpture above the north door of Quenington's church

Carvings on the font in Southrop's ancient church reveal much about the arms and armour of Stephen's time

Bampton church, a retreat for Matilda's garrison in 1142

St Stephen's, Clanfield

of its fabric appear to be incorporated in the present church tower. After passing through **Clanfield**, the royal troops also forced the surrender of a garrison at **Radcot**, then a hamlet rendered difficult of access by watercourses and marshes adjoining the Thames. Thence Stephen probably marched through **Faringdon** and followed the line of the Thames most of the way to **Oxford**, where he apparently arrived near the end of September. A grimly determined Stephen, in the midst of a strong force of cavalry and infantry, probably gazed down on the city from Hinksey Hill. The previous year Matilda had easily gained control of Oxford, when Stephen's commanders there, an earl and a baron, had changed their allegiance – they were, according to the king's biographer "effeminate men, whose endowment lay rather in wanton delights than in resolution of mind". But now, his biographer intimated, Stephen had a tough nut to crack: "Oxford is a city very securely protected, inaccessible because of the very deep water that washes it all round, most carefully encircled by the palisade of an outwork on one side [the city ramparts] and on another finely and very strongly fortified by an impregnable castle and a tower of great height." Moreover, Robert of Gloucester had recently stiffened the defences with additional earthworks. Despite a bad fire in the city in 1138, Matilda could levy the manpower and resources of one of the most prosperous trading communities in England, with its gilds of weavers and shoemakers, and commercial links stretching through London to Lorraine. The surviving crypt of St Peter in the East, on the east side of Queen's Lane, gives a glimpse of the aspirations and fears of an ambitious bourgeois society. Capitals are finely sculpted and there is a relic chamber, such as are found in continental churches. If the church already housed particularly prized relics in 1142, their presence failed to help avert the disaster which was to overwhelm the city that autumn.

Matilda remained in Oxford confident in the high quality of her soldiers, the strength of the city's defences, and her control of resources in the surrounding regions. She had a garrison at Woodstock, a favourite country seat of her father's, and one at the enormously strong castle at Wallingford (Berkshire), from which she could control navigation on the Thames south of Oxford. But she reckoned without the determination of Stephen and the offensive spirit of his men, who had enjoyed a series of easy successes and a campaign in well-stocked country. The royal army almost certainly approached the city from the south, along the Abingdon Road and across the fords and causeways which led to the main crossing of the Thames (now marked by Folly Bridge) and which carried on towards the South Gate of the city. Matilda's forces came out from behind its ramparts to oppose Stephen, concentrating on the river bank, presumably to cover the causeway across the main stream. They hurled insults at Stephen's men on the opposite bank, and picked them off with some effective archery. But the king was shown "an old, extremely deep ford": and his biographer describes how, like a hero of chivalrous epics, he plunged in among the foremost, "swimming rather than wading" to the other bank – no mean feat in armour. This move caught the defenders off-balance. Perhaps they were outflanked by the king getting unexpectedly through shallow water away from the main causeway. He and his companions pursued them as

BAMPTON Oxfordshire
SP 315035 OS 164
Bampton (also called Bampton-in-the-Bush) is five miles south-south-west of Witney, on the A4095. The large church of St Mary includes Norman work, and the tower stormed by Stephen's men: but it is mainly of the thirteenth and fourteenth centuries, with much of interest within. Half a mile to the west, in Mill Street, stand the gatehouse and other remains of fourteenth century Bampton Castle, incorporated into the later buildings of Ham House: and the large Cotswold-stone village also possesses several other notable mansions, mainly Georgian.

CLANFIELD Oxfordshire
SP 284022 OS 163
Clanfield is four miles north of Faringdon on the A4095. Stephen's army passed through here on the way between Bampton and Radcot. The parish church, dedicated to St Stephen, has a medieval carving of the saint on the tower.

RADCOT Oxfordshire
SU 285995 OS 163
Radcot is three miles north of Faringdon on the A4095. Radcot Bridge is the oldest remaining bridge over the Thames, dating probably from the fourteenth century. Stephen's army probably crossed the river here: and in December 1387 the bridge was the site of a battle wherein Robert de Vere, Earl of Oxford and chief supporter of Richard II, was routed by the rebellious Lords Appellant and Henry Bolingbroke (later Henry IV)

FARINGDON Berkshire
SU 288958 OS 163
Faringdon is eleven miles north-east of Swindon. Stephen's army probably went here from Radcot. His biographer describes how in 1145 Robert Earl of Gloucester advanced to the hamlet of Faringdon, "a delightful spot abounding in all sorts of supplies" and built a castle there, garrisoning it with his best troops in order to curb the sorties made by the king's garrisons in and around Oxford. But Stephen advanced on Faringdon and forced the surrender of the castle by what his biographer considered a masterpiece of siegecraft. The castle has completely disappeared: but the parish church contains Norman work, and within are medieval brasses and fine Tudor monuments to the Unton family.

OXFORD

SP 513063 OS 164

*The defences of Oxford date from the late
ninth or early tenth century when the town
was part of the West Saxon defence
system against the Danes. The defences
were enlarged in the early eleventh century
in response to the renewed Danish
invasions. New stone defences were built
in the thirteenth century: stone walls and
semi-circular bastions were largely
completed in the period 1226–40. The
best remaining section of walls and towers
are in New College gardens.*

*Oxford Castle was founded by Robert
de Oilli in 1071. He was presumably
responsible for the earthworks of the motte
and bailey. The chapel of St George was
founded in the castle in 1074. Pillars from
its crypt are now incorporated in a later
cellar. If the crypt was there in 1142, it was
probably used for storing victuals in the
siege and may have been a refuge for
Matilda and her ladies during
bombardments.*

*Being within the bounds of Oxford
Prison, the castle is only accessible by
special arrangement, but can be seen from
New Road and Tidmarsh Lane. There is
also much else to see in Oxford, including
the many colleges; the Bodleian Library
(Broad Street); Christ Church Cathedral
(in St Aldates); the University Church of
St Mary (High Street); St Michael-at-the-
Northgate, with its Saxon tower
(Cornmarket Street); and the fine Norman
crypt of St Peter's-in-the-East (Queen's
Lane).*

far as the city gates – presumably the South Gate, which lay across what is now St Aldate's, near the present facade of Christ Church, south of Tom Tower. Then, when the main body of the royal army had crossed the river (presumably by the main causeway), a full-scale attack was launched which drove Matilda's forces in confusion back through the city gates. The king's men slipped inside too, mingling with the enemy in small groups, and spreading confusion in the city by hurling firebrands into houses. The defence disintegrated as Stephen's forces slew and captured those who continued to resist; others fled from the city amidst the plundering and burning. Some of them doubtless streamed through the North Gate past the nearby tower of St Michael's church, which may have been built in the mid-eleventh century to strengthen the ramparts. This surviving Saxon tower was probably one of the few structures in a busy commercial area to remain intact after the sack, because of its stone construction. The fall of Oxford took place on the 26th of September.

However, knights of Matilda's household, together with some of the soldiers fleeing from the rout, guarded her safely in the castle, which was quickly surrounded by Stephen's men. The castle's main defensive features in 1142 are still there – the massive mound and St George's Tower, rightly described by Stephen's biographer as the "tower of great height". Despite the time of year, the king was determined to mount a siege of the castle until he captured his rival: in fact the siege turned out to be an epic one, lasting probably for nearly three months into a particularly severe winter. The intrepid Matilda endured bombardment by siege-engines and dwindling food supplies. She had, indeed, some hopes of relief. Nobles who were ashamed of having deserted her assembled a force at Wallingford. But since Stephen was reputed to have over 1,000 knights, many of whom had flocked to him for the pickings of Oxford, his opponents were not prepared to attack him in the city. Then Robert of Gloucester arrived back from Normandy. He had Matilda's little boy (the future Henry II) with him but had failed to get the count of Anjou to come, and he had with him only between three and four hundred knights. But Robert audaciously seized Wareham harbour and town and besieged the castle there, hoping that Stephen would be diverted to relieve it. For three precious weeks he impatiently maintained the siege; until, when it became clear to Stephen's knights that there was no hope of relief, they surrendered. Robert did not then head for Wallingford in order to attack Stephen in Oxford, but summoned an assembly of forces further off at Cirencester for the beginning of December. The supporters of Matilda who had assembled at Wallingford had probably had to disperse; Cirencester may have been a more convenient assembly-point for her supporters, and one at which increasingly scarce supplies could be more rapidly accumulated from Bristol and other western bases. But when the force set out eastwards from Cirencester its progress was probably slowed down by the cold and ice and snow. Matilda's garrison, meanwhile, was near the end of its supplies – she was in despair. But the news that Robert was in the field demoralised Stephen's men too. They were probably also miserable with cold and hunger, their plight exacerbated by the earlier destruction in the city. The transport of supplies to them along the Thames was hampered by ice on the river, besides the presence of Matilda's garrison at Wallingford. There were desertions: those who remained became more preoccupied with preparing their defences against Robert than the round-the clock watch on the castle. This slackness was noted by the garrison. One night shortly before Christmas, Matilda, with between three and five knights, was either lowered from the castle by ropes or slipped out of a postern. They got past Stephen's men without detection. A heavy fall of snow muffled their steps and ice probably facilitated their crossing of the castle ditch. They had camouflaged themselves by wrapping up in white linen (probably the bedsheets of Matilda and her ladies). The journey south-wards to the river was probably as hazardous as getting out of the castle, for it is likely that the king had watches in this vicinity to guard against the anticipated approach of Earl Robert. The fugitives crossed the Thames, thickly iced over, at the place where Stephen had waded across in September. Matilda remained "dry-footed, without wetting her clothes at all". On the other bank "the blaring of trumpeters" and "the cries of men shouting loudly", the king's watches keeping in touch, rapidly receded in the silence of night. Matilda and her knights had a gruelling walk of six miles to Abingdon: there horses were available and she rode straight on to the safety of Wallingford Castle. The knights whom she had left behind in Oxford Castle soon surrendered to a chastened Stephen. Robert diverted his advance for a joyful reunion with his sister at Wallingford. On her advice, the forces were dismissed. It was not the time of year to campaign, not least because men thought it right to refrain from warfare in the holy season of Christmas and to rest and celebrate in their own homes with their kinsfolk and habitual companions.

Matilda's escape appeared miraculous to contemporaries. The complete success within Stephen's grasp after a brilliant and determined campaign had eluded him. But he continued to hold the great prize of Oxford during the fighting which was to be frequently renewed during the remaining twelve years of his reign. His possession of it was a barrier to the extension of Matilda's influence eastwards. It was a base from which his forces could raid and set up garrisons to the west. But Matilda's garrison at Wallingford remained a solitary thorn in Stephen's side, despite his determined efforts to excise it. The rivals' long occupation of these bases close to one another in the Thames valley suggests that there was a degree of prosperity in the region sustaining their garrisons: the period was not one of universal devastation and want. But people found the continuing presence of the soldiery a burden on their not very elastic agrarian resources. They hated the threat of insecurity, which the troublesome garrisons did little to allay: what had happened at Oxford in 1142 might happen again as long as there was a force in the rival allegiance not many miles down the river.

Stephen and his principal opponents showed themselves at their best on the campaign of 1142, accomplishing heroic deeds intrepidly. But both sides failed in 1142 – and foreshadowed their future failures. Even though the fields of operation that year were not far from some of their principal bases, they were unable to concentrate the forces in the realm nominally under their control sufficiently for a knock-out blow.

King John
The King's last raid
KING'S LYNN–NEWARK 1216

John Steane

John (1166–1216) was born at Oxford, the youngest child of Henry II and Eleanor of Aquitaine. He succeeded his brother Richard I in 1199. John's kingship was controversial among contemporaries and remains so. There were spectacular crises. In 1204 the king of France seized his duchy of Normandy. In 1208 Pope Innocent III placed England under an Interdict, suspending church services. In 1214 John's efforts to recover his lost French lands, exasperatingly expensive to his subjects in England, were checked by the defeat of his allies at Bouvines. Next year he sealed Magna Carta, in order to head off rebellion by winning over moderate baronial opinion. The charter was a detailed indictment of some aspects of royal government as it had developed since the Conquest, and an affirmation of others. For the first time an English king agreed that subjects should coerce him if he failed to observe rules for kingship. But John soon repudiated the charter and was campaigning brilliantly against rebels when he died of dysentery at Newark. He left a son aged nine to succeed him, Henry III. John's tomb can be seen in Worcester Cathedral.

John was short and stout. He was a luxurious dresser, a gourmet and womaniser. Besides possessing the celebrated furious temper of the House of Anjou, he had a sardonic sense of humour. He liked hunting, gambling and reading romances. He was highly intelligent, a keen administrator, perceptive judge and inventive politician. His familiars served him well, but he failed to form trusting relationships with his magnates.

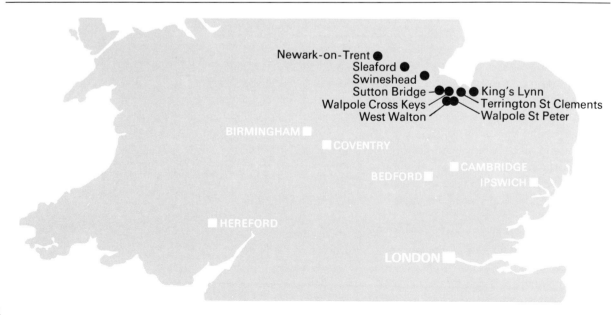

King John has not had a good press from the chroniclers and historians. Matthew Paris, the monkish historian of St Albans abbey (writing thirty years after the event) is largely responsible for the traditional impression. He regarded John as "a tyrant, not a king, a destroyer instead of a governor, crushing his own people and favouring aliens, a lion to his subjects, but a lamb to foreigners and rebels. He had lost the duchy of Normandy and many other territories through sloth, and was actually keen to lose the kingdom of England or to ruin it. He was an insatiable extorter of money" ... and so on. In addition Matthew Paris makes out that John was a libidinous lecher and a glutton, who preyed on other mens' wives and daughters and was unstable and unfaithful in religion. This view commended itself to Victorian historians. "Foul as it is", wrote J R Green, "Hell itself is defiled by the fouler presence of King John". Modern historians, while still maintaining that his character was flawed and that he was revengeful and petty minded, also realise that he possessed "the high administrative ability of a great ruler" (Warren). It is illuminating to watch the king during the last few months of his life, and to see whether there are clues there which will support one or other of these judgements.

John was undoubtedly faced with problems of appalling complexity at the beginning of 1216. His throne had rocked on a swelling tide of disaffection for the last four years. He had upset the baronage by his loss of Normandy; he had been outmanoeuvred by the French king Philip Augustus into losing the bulk of his continental possessions; and he had gained, perhaps unfairly, the reputation of being John "Softsword" – for although he had a flair for imaginative strategy, he lacked boldness. He had certainly stretched the financial sources that antiquated feudal custom allowed him to their limit: gaining himself a reputation for extortion and greed. He had quarrelled with the Papacy and earned excommunication for himself and an Interdict – or total suspension of all church services – for his kingdom. Despite his reconciliation with Rome, he had been faced with baronial opposition which had culminated in Magna Carta. This was less a charter of liberties than a baronial document giving a detailed commentary on the abuses of Angevin government. Finally, he was faced with open rebellion and foreign invasion. England, in 1216, was torn by civil war and the prey of Scots and marauding foreign mercenaries: and in May Prince Louis of France – offered the crown by the rebel barons – landed at the head of a French army, so that within a short time almost the whole of eastern England fell into the hands of John's enemies.

By the end of the summer of 1216, however, the situation had improved somewhat from the king's point of view. While two thirds of the barons had sided with Louis, those in the west of England stood firm for the crown: and a number of castles in key positions, such as Windsor and Dover, also remained loyal to the king. "Day by day the adherents of the Frenchmen dwindled", and although the king of Scots had made contact with Louis, there was a chance to head him off before he returned to his own kingdom.

The last journey of John shows no diminution of the extraordinary powers of energy and activity which, like his father Henry II and brother Richard I before him, he could summon when necessary. Throughout his reign "he was in motion ceaselessly, carrying his scrutiny into the west, and

The profile of Corfe Castle which welcomes the traveller today would have been an awesome sight for any invading foe

into the far north where kings seldom came" (Joliffe). An indication of the speed the court could move is seen in the year 1200, when it was at Marlborough on the 19th of November and by the 23rd of the same month had arrived at Lincoln, a distance of about 150 miles. In fact it very frequently travelled between thirty-five and forty miles a day, and on particular occasions fifty miles. During 1204–5 John is recorded as having made 360 moves, visiting 145 royal manors or properties, 129 castles and forty-six religious houses as well as forty other houses. Well might Matthew Paris sum it up *"Citius quam credi fas est"*. – "He was swifter than you would have believed possible."

We are reminded of Walter Map's complaints about John's father, Henry II "he was always on the move, travelling in unbearably long stages, like a post, and in this respect merciless beyond measure to the household that accompanied him . . . We used to ascribe his exertions, not to fickleness, but to his fear of growing fat". Peter of Blois similarly groaned about this "bustling, scrambling, roving pandemonium" (Norgate's phrase) and said "if the king has promised to spend a day in a place, you may be quite sure he will upset everybody's arrangement by starting off early in the morning. Then you may see men rushing about as if they were mad, beating their packhorses, driving their wagons into one another. In short, such a turmoil as to present you with a lively image of the infernal regions".

On Louis' landing in Kent, John retreated to Winchester; then, by way of Ludgershall, Devizes, Wilton, Sturminster and Wareham, he fell back on Corfe Castle, where he remained from the 23rd to the 17th of July. The magnificent ruins of the castle, sited in a gap in the Purbeck ridge, still dominate the little town of Corfe. The craftsmen here were already famous in the thirteenth century for the production of Purbeck marble, a dark and gleaming material exported all over the country for pillars, effigies and tombs. John had spent considerable sums on making his favourite Corfe Castle safer earlier in the reign; and he was also responsible for building a magnificent series of chambers known as the "Gloriette" which were of the highest architectural quality, reflecting an elegant mode of life. Corfe was John's treasury and in the castle he stored valuables and money. Here he collected a considerable army, chiefly drawn from the garrisons of his castles, and proceeded on a fearsome journey spreading havoc at harvest time among the estates of his enemies the rebel earls and barons, burning their houses and destroying their crops. He set out from Corfe on the 18th of July and called in the next day at Sherborne in northern Dorset. Here are the extensive remains of a castle built by Roger, Bishop of Salisbury (1107–1135) which was in crown hands during John's reign. The surviving curtain wall and central keep would have been seen by the king. From here he traversed Somerset to Bristol, already in the early thirteenth century an important port for routes to Ireland and south-west France. Next he made his way to Gloucester (21st of July) Tewkesbury, Hereford, Shrewsbury, Whitchurch and the marches of Wales, where he stayed a fortnight. We can follow his route by checking the stream of writs which were being issued by the chancery office accompanying the rapidly-moving king. Each one, patiently copied by the clerks into the Close Rolls, briefly records the place and date of the attestation. This rich documentary record never diminishes despite the increasing strains of civil war, and there are no signs that the king's intellectual powers or ruthless will were faltering during these last few weeks of his life.

John finally returned to Corfe on the 25th of August, but not to rest. The next day he set off for Windsor. His furious speed again reminds us of Walter Map's rueful comments on the breakneck activity of his father, Henry II. Since the castles of Old Sarum and Marlborough had already been surrendered to Louis by their castellan, his route was a roundabout one via Sherborne and Wells. Here the cathedral had been under construction since 1180: during the Interdict (1209–1212) all work had ceased, and when the carpenters and masons took up their tools again there is a noticeable change in carpentry techniques in the roof structure of the nave. By the 28th of August John had reached Bath, and from there he turned eastwards along the line of the A4 to Bradford-on-Avon and Chippenham. On the 2nd of September he marched up from Cirencester to Burford. This was sheep country, and along the top of the bare Cotswolds roamed the great flocks belonging to religious houses such as Winchcombe and Minchinhampton. Their fleeces went to swell the cargoes of what was the most important English export of the thirteenth century. From Burford he followed the course of the present A40 to Oxford, where he spent the next three days. These were early days in the life of the nascent university, and the town was still at the height of its commercial prosperity before obstruction on the Thames began to drain its life. Oxford Castle had been dumped by William I over a quadrant of the Anglo-Saxon "burh", or defended settlement. Substantial parts which King John would have seen still remain. The massive grass-grown mound which overshadows the County Council offices and the prison, was originally crowned with a keep. Below, on one side of the bailey, is the tapering St George's tower of early Norman construction, which houses an eleventh-century crypt in its base.

After spending three days in Oxford the king struck across the Thames to Wallingford, which he reached on the 5th of September. This town, walled with Saxon earth ramparts, was at an historic river crossing forded by William I in his march after Hastings which aimed to encircle London. The ford had been replaced by a new multi-arched bridge of flint and stone dating from the twelfth century; and remains of this are embedded in the later medieval structure. Wallingford Castle, once one of the most impressive English earthen and stone fortresses, has been reduced to some mounds, ditches and fragments of masonry in a field overlooking the river. From here it was quite a short march through the Goring gap to Reading. The king stayed nearby at the palace of the bishops of Salisbury at Sonning. Unfortunately this was demolished in the sixteenth century, but the site is south of the church. Its foundations were excavated in 1912–14.

His advance to Sonning certainly looked as if he intended to relieve Windsor, but in fact when he moved it was to attempt to intercept the Scots King Alexander on his homeward journey, after he had come to England to do homage to Louis. On September the 15th he suddenly struck northwards from Walton-on-Thames to Aylesbury and Bedford, which he reached within a day. The next day he travelled thirty miles to Cambridge so that part of his forces straddled Alexander's route homewards. The rest went on another *chevauchée* or mounted raid, ravaging the land of the rebel barons in Norfolk and Suffolk. As Roger of Wendover put it, "*misera afflictione contrivit*" – he contrived lamentable damage. The king was still in Cambridge on the 17th of September, but on the next day he appeared before Robert de Vere's Castle at Hedingham in northern Essex. Its gaunt tower keep is one of the mightiest fortifications of the twelfth century. The barons, in the meanwhile, raised the siege of Windsor Castle, burned their siege engines, and hurried after John hoping to make him prisoner. But in one day he moved twenty-six miles, and then marched from Cambridge to Stamford, a distance of forty miles.

He next appeared briefly at Kingscliffe, west of Peterborough, a royal house and hunting lodge in the Forest of Rockingham. This was close to the church, and near the field called Hall Yard. Stone foundations and quantities of ash have been discovered which were probably part of the lodge. Though this was a favourite Angevin hunting base, John needed a more defensive position, and he pushed on to the squat towers of William of Aumale's castle at Rockingham. On the 21st of September he arrived in the rich lands of the valley of the Nene, which were owned by the rebel monks of the abbey of Peterborough, and he burned their houses and barns around Oundle. He then marched on to Crowland Abbey, north of Peterborough, and bade his mercenary captain Savaric de Mauléon fire the abbey church. It is said that Savaric yielded to a large money offer from the monks and desisted from this sacrilege, but the implacable king heaped his lieutenant with abuse and helped with his own hands to fire the harvest fields, running up and down amid the smoke and flames. A fragment, at any rate, of Crowland Abbey still stands – largely wrecked by John's successor Henry VIII, three hundred and seventy years later. John then continued to march north and relieved the royal garrison at Lincoln before wasting with fire and sword the Isle of Axholme. He passed through parts of Lindsey and Holland in Lincolnshire to Grimsby, and thence south again to Spalding. Roger of Wendover describes the Lincolnshire fields all white to harvest, and since it was by now the first week of October the harvest must have been late this year. These fields, with the houses and buildings, were fired by this terrible army of marauding mercenaries with the king at its head.

It is not clear why he next marched to **King's Lynn**, but evidently he was received there with loyalty and affection by the burghers, who gave him a considerable money grant. By the beginning of the thirteenth century Lynn was already one of the greatest ports of medieval England, exporting the wool and corn from its rich hinterland to the Netherlands, the Rhineland and the Baltic countries and receiving in return, timber, pitch, honey and wax. The burghers sumptuously entertained John, who feasted until his excesses brought on a violent attack of dysentery. Far from resting, however, John moved next day to Wisbech.

To understand the next event, we must recall that the medieval coastline hereabouts was in the thirteenth century several miles further inland than at present, though already generations of peasant farmers had been engaged in reclaiming the fen and silt lands, by building seabanks to keep out the salt waters of the Wash. To make his way north, John had to cross

KING'S LYNN Norfolk
TF 620195 OS 132
On the A47 twelve miles north-east of Wisbech. An important medieval outport for northern Norfolk and the rich Fenland. Two market places, the so-called Tuesday and Saturday Market Places, and two magnificent parish churches. Plenty of reminders of the prosperous mercantile past, with Guildhall, Hampton Court, Hanseatic warehouses, remains of the city walls and Southgate. See also Lynn Museum (Market St), Museum of Social History, St George's Guildhall.

TERRINGTON ST CLEMENTS Norfolk
TF 552205 OS 131
*On the A17 six miles to west of King's
Lynn. A magnificent marshland church,
Perpendicular throughout, a mark of the
great wealth in corn and wool of the Fens.*

WALPOLE ST PETER Norfolk
TF 503168 OS 131
*Two miles north of the A47 between
Wisbech and King's Lynn. An outstanding
marshland church with screenwork, stalls
and benches all of fifteenth century date.
A mile to the north is the winding sea bank
which marks the edge of the medieval
coast.*

WEST WALTON Norfolk
TF 472134 OS 131
*Two miles north of Wisbech, a splendid
marshland church of thirteenth century
date with a notable detached tower*

WALPOLE CROSS KEYS Norfolk
TF 514200 OS 131
*The western end of the road from Lynn to
the crossing of the Well Stream in the
middle ages. From here westwards,
following roughly the present line of the
A17 and the disused railway track, was the
crossing, four miles long.*

SUTTON BRIDGE Lincolnshire
TF 483210 OS 131
*The approximate point where the loss of
King John's baggage train occurred.*

the Ouse (at this time a wide estuary) by ferry and to travel through the villages of **Terrington St Clement** and **Walpole St Andrew**. Thence he would follow the course of the old seabank to **West Walton** (the place name "wall" in these villages refers of course to the seabank or wall) and so to Wisbech. Here he could cross the river called the Well Stream. He stayed the night at Wisbech castle and then journeyed north into Lincolnshire, passing along the west side of the Well Stream through Newton, Tydd St Mary, Long Sutton and Holbeach. In the meantime, his baggage train had orders to follow him on a more direct line. From Terrington St Clement, their road went westwards to **Walpole Cross Keys**. Here the Well Stream in the thirteenth century was four and a half miles wide. At low water there was a passage over the sands between Cross Keys and Long Sutton, across which guides carrying a pole or staff conducted horses and carriages. Along this route came the cumbersome baggage train of the king – sumpter horses, wagons, carts carrying tents, the heavier military equipment, engines of war, treasure chests, the king's wardrobe and chapel and the other *impedimenta* of a considerable army.

They had left Lynn about midday on the 11th, and could not have reached the estuary until within an hour or two of high water. The falling tide left the estuary dry some distance from the bank, and it is possible that October mists prevented them from seeing the state of the retreating waters. At any rate, according to the chronicler Coggeshall, "they incautiously and precipitantly pressed on before the tide had receded", while Paris wrote "they ventured to cross without a guide". It is likely that, on reaching the sands, they no longer kept to the single or double line dictated by a narrow country road but spread out, and were soon floundering in quicksands. The confused mass of struggling and shouting people were overwhelmed by the turning tide. It is likely too, that the doomed men, vehicles and horses would go on sinking until a firmer stratum was reached. There is a ballast bed twenty-three feet below the silt, and here probably lies King John's treasure in the region of **Sutton Bridge**!

Historians debate how much was lost. The well attested fact that the king was grief stricken at the disaster seems to suggest that he had lost all his treasure. When he had embarked on his career of harrying after the Magna Carta, he had secured possession of his valuables by calling them in from the monasteries and the bishops where he had previously dispersed them for safekeeping. Within a month he had gathered 143 cups and fourteen goblets, fourteen dishes, eight flagons, five pairs of basins, forty belts, six clasps, sixteen staffs, fifty-two rings and two pendants, four shrines, two gold crosses, three gold combs, a gold vessel ornamented with pearls, two candelabra, two thuribles and three golden phylacteries. The cups were mostly of white silver, but ten were of silver gilt, and one was jewelled with sapphires. The staffs were of great magnificence, studded with rubies, sapphires, diamonds, garnets, a heliotrope, topazes and emeralds, and the rings were chiefly set with rubies and sapphires. In addition there was the coronation regalia, of which the king possessed two sets, the second being described as belonging to the "Lady Empress" – his grandmother Matilda, Stephen's opponent. Usually these were in the keeping of the Knights Templars or Knights Hospitallers, but we know that they had recently been handed back

St Margaret's in Saturday Market Place, and below, the Corn Exchange building in Tuesday Market Place; both in King's Lynn

The tower stands aloof from the body of its church in West Walton

A dry sea bank no longer wet-nurses land stolen from the Wash

Marshland landscapes near Walpole
Cross Keys

Is King John's treasure buried beneath Sutton Bridge?

The Bishop of Lincoln's castle at Newark, by the Trent

SWINESHEAD Lincolnshire
TF 249408 OS 131
The site of Swineshead Abbey is one mile north-east of the village on a private estate, flanked on one side by the A52. A house (1607) is built from remains of the Cistercian Abbey founded in 1135.

SLEAFORD Lincolnshire
TF 069455 OS 130
Earthworks in Westgate playing-field at the back of the town are all that remain to indicate the site of the castle of Bishop Alexander of Lincoln, who also built castles at Newark and Banbury. Splendid fourteenth century church.

NEWARK-ON-TRENT Nottinghamshire
SK 797540 OS 121
On the A46 seventeen miles south-west of Lincoln. The castle built by Bishop Alexander of Lincoln is situated on a cliff along the river. John would have passed throught the north gateway. The south-west angle tower and the crypt are of the twelfth century. See Millgate Museum of Social and Folk Life, Newark District Council Museum.

to the king. Those surrendered by the Hospitallers in March 1216 included a wand of gold with a cross, belts and nine great necklaces set with precious stones, a royal tunic of red samite with embroideries and precious stones, and so on. It seems highly likely that all this was lost in the disaster, because when John's son Henry III was crowned on Whit Sunday 1220 it was noticeable that the rich regalia of his father was absent. A few old sandals, some buskins, an ancient pallium (robe) and some swords from Corfe were all that could be assembled.

The king's sickness was, moreover, aggravated by the disaster: but he struggled on and reached **Swineshead** abbey near Boston, where rage and grief threw him into a fever. Roger of Wendover, nevertheless, describes him as supping greedily on peaches and new cider. Certainly John had a reputation of being a voracious glutton. He once gave alms to a hundred paupers "because he ate twice on Friday on the eve of St Mark" and in church would send to the preacher bidding him to conclude the sermon as he wanted his dinner. And what dinners! For the Christmas feast at Winchester in 1206 he ordered 1,500 chickens, 5,000 eggs, twenty oxen, 100 pigs and 100 sheep.

The effect of the peaches and cider on a frame weakened by dysentery and incessant travel was mortal. With great difficulty he made his way on the 14th to **Sleaford**, one of the castles of the bishops of Lincoln, where the king suffered a fresh attack of fever which bleeding failed to relieve. But nothing would calm his restlessness, and he again set out on horseback on the 16th of October. After he had ridden only three or four miles, "panting and groaning", he was forced to dismount and had his followers make him a litter – the best they could do was to hack the willows at the side of the road and weave a hammock, over which they flung a horsecloth. In this the wretched king was slung between two of the high-mettled destriers of his knights. "This accursed litter has broken all my bones and well nigh killed me" cried the king in his pain and rage.

By the time he reached the Bishop of Lincoln's Castle at **Newark-on-Trent**, he was dying. The Abbot of Croxton ministered to his body and soul, persuading him to confess his sins and receive communion. Even in the throes of death, John showed a remarkably cool and efficient grasp of detail. He left a simple but straightforward will; solemnly declared his son Henry his heir; made those round him swear an oath to the boy; sent letters to the sheriffs and castellans bidding them to recognise him as their lord; and (a sure sign of excellent judgement) sent word to William the Marshal, the great and unflinchingly loyal Earl of Pembroke, placing young Henry in his care.

When the Abbot of Croxton asked him where he wished to be buried, the king replied "I commend my body and my soul to God and St. Wulfstan" (the patron saint of Worcester). On the night of his death, October the 18th, a whirlwind swept over Newark and the townsfolk thought their houses would fall. The king had donated his heart and a hundred shillings' worth of land to Croxton Abbey – south-west of Grantham – and the abbot swiftly possessed himself of the grisly relic, embalmed the body, and fled. The body was dressed in such scraps of regalia as were left, and his remaining soldiers, in full armour, conveyed the royal corpse right across war-torn

England to St. Wulfstan's cathedral at Worcester. Here John was buried by Bishop Silvester. In 1232 a magnificent effigy of Purbeck marble was erected by his son, our only portrait of the king. Three centuries later in 1528 his remains were disinterred. The translation of the inscription made at the time reads as follows.

"Masons in the building of another sepulchre
Where now, behold he lies, found the body decayed
But nevertheless adorned with a sword and a crown on the head
The right hand holding a fair rod and the left a sceptre.
Next (to the body) came a golden vestment which a silk one covered
A spur was on his foot, a ring on his finger,
Therefore whoever thou art who readest this inscription
Say 'omnipotent Father look with favour on thy servant John'".

Edward I
The invasion of Wales
WORCESTER–CONWY 1282/3

John Steane

Edward I (1239–1307) was the son of Henry III and Eleanor of Provence. He gained his political and military apprenticeship in the baronial conflicts of his father's reign. After Edward's succession in 1272, he instituted major legal reforms and suppressed the remains of Welsh independence. But his high-handed application of the principle that the English Crown was sovereign in the British Isles provoked the Scottish Wars of Independence. In the 1290's demands for aid against the Scots and for war with France, which his subjects regarded as excessive and arbitrary, produced an atmosphere of political confrontation which rebounded on his son Edward II. Edward I died at Burgh by Sands preparing once more to crush the rebellious Scots.

Edward was tall and elegant with a drooping eyelid and a slight lisp. He expected obedience and had a furious temper – he once threw his daughter's coronet on the fire. He was a crusader, a patron of chivalry, a connoisseur of horseflesh and a keen falconer. He enjoyed lying in bed late in the morning and eating good suppers, playing chess and dice, being entertained by minstrels, buffoons and tumblers. Some thought him an ungenerous master and a treacherous adversary.

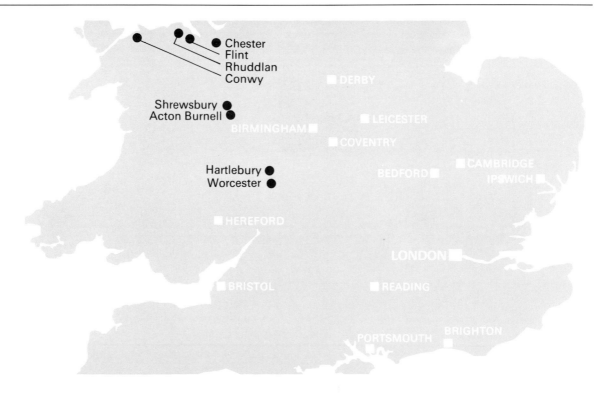

Throughout the period 1066–1284 English kings attempted from time to time to obtain administrative and military control of Wales. The terrain was difficult; rugged mountains, dense woods and steep valleys, fought over by native princes and marcher lords. The land became studded with their castles and these fortresses were the ultimate arbiters of war and peace. By the second half of the twelfth century the rulers of Deheubarth in south-west Wales, (particularly the lord Rhys) and of Gwynedd emerged as power-ful rulers. The princes of the north-western kingdom of Gwynedd based their power on their natural stronghold of Snowdonia and their control over the agricultural grain lands of Anglesey. In the thirteenth century two rulers of Gwynedd, both outstanding personalities, Llywelyn ap Iorwerth (the Great) and his grandson Llywelyn ap Gruffydd (the Last), managed to rally the whole nation round them and to bring all other Welsh dynasties under their authority. A clash over the homage claimed from the unruly Llywelyn ap Gruffydd by the punctilious and unrelenting English king Edward I, led to war in July 1277. Edward's success in this war left four new English royal castles as advanced military bases in Wales. These – Aberystwyth, Builth, Flint and Rhuddlan – were made of wood to start with and now were to be completed in stone with all possible speed. Moreover Llywelyn was stripped of most of his former rights and possessions and was forced to render homage to Edward. His brother Dafydd, who had changed sides four times, was given a smaller part of Llywelyn's lands in Snowdonia than he thought he deserved or had been promised. These grievances led to an increasing tension, which erupted into the revolt of the two brothers. In March 1282, therefore, the English crown was thus faced once again with the problem of conquering Wales.

Edward summoned a council at Devizes in Wiltshire on April the 5th 1282 to take measures to counter the rebellion. He began by appointing the Earl of Gloucester commander-in-chief in the South. The crisis facing him was graphically described in a letter he sent to Margaret Queen of France, in which he begged to be excused from sending to her the subsidy which he had promised for her war in Provence. He explained that he needed all his resources for the war which Llywelyn and his brother Dafydd were waging against him in Wales. Roger de Clifford had been taken prisoner, many men had been slain and one of the king's castles in that region had been occupied (this was Hawarden Castle, near Chester). His whole army was needed to put down the rebellion.

The events of the next few weeks are a fascinating record of the speed and efficiency with which Edward raised his forces and led them against the Welsh. The ships of the Cinque Ports of Kent and Sussex were sum-moned. They would be needed to conduct amphibious operations along the north Welsh coast. The royal castles of Flint and Rhuddlan, which were desperately holding out, could be supplied by sea, and sea power would also aid in the conquest of Anglesey, the island granary of the Welsh. The crown tenants were "affectionately requested" to come to Worcester by May the 17th, thence to accompany the king "at our wages". These would be provided, to the tune of 12,000 marks, by royal borrowing from various Italian firms. Agents were sent to Ireland and Scotland to obtain corn, fish, iron, salt and other supplies, and wine was also sought from Gascony and

A ruinous appendage to Shrewsbury Abbey

The north-facing side of the Abbey, crowded by a massive beech

One of Shrewsbury Castle's towers perched high above the River Severn

The neat appearance of the Rows in Chester owes much to reconstruction work carried out in the nineteenth century

Stonework in Chester's Roman amphitheatre, capable, it is said, of seating many thousands of spectators

Flint Castle once commanded the estuary of the River Dee

The particularly well-preserved structure of Rhuddlan Castle includes a fortified
dock which was once fed from the River Clwyd

WORCESTER Hereford and Worcester
SO 851545 OS 150
*On the A38, eight miles north-east of
Great Malvern. The cathedral has
transepts, a circular chapter house and
frater (all Norman) a chancel of the
thirteenth century and a crossing tower of
1374. King John's tomb is in the chancel.
The Bishops' Palace has some work of
Bishop Giffard's time. Nothing much is left
of the castle, originally a motte-and-bailey
... "now clene down" (Leland 1538), St
Alban's, St Andrew's and St John's
churches all have medieval work and are
worth visiting. Worcester also has the
Commandery (a fifteenth century building
with museum), City Museum and Art
Gallery (Foregate St.) and the Tudor
House (Friar St.)*

HARTLEBURY Hereford and Worcester
SP 836713 OS 138
*On the A449 from Kidderminster to
Worcester, three miles south of
Kidderminster. The castle was begun by
Bishop Walter de Cantelupe c.1255, and
Bishop Giffard fortified it in 1268. Part
of the moat remains from the time of
Edward I's visit. Fine fifteenth century great
hall. The Hereford and Worcester county
museum has displays of country crafts and
industries.*

ACTON BURNELL Shropshire
ST 534018 OS 126
*Eight miles south of Shrewsbury, between
the A49 and the A458. Fortified and
embattled house of Bishop Robert Burnell.
Remains of medieval barn. St Mary's
church has much thirteenth century work.*

SHREWSBURY Shropshire
SJ 494128 OS 126
*On the A5 twelve miles west of Telford.
Dramatic site "standeth on a rocky hill of
stone" (Leland). Among medieval
buildings are the abbey and St Mary's
church. Remains of thirteenth century
town walls and castle. This was built by
Roger of Montgomery in 1102: Henry III
added round towers and Edward I the hall.
Also see fragments of three houses
(Vaughan's Mansion; Music Hall; Benets
Hall, Pride Hill). Charles Darwin's
birthplace, Clive House Museum,
Pumping Station Museum, Viroconium
Roman city (five miles to south east).*

Ponthieu, now part of the inheritance of Queen Eleanor, Edward's wife. Meanwhile, as a result of the king's call, within three months a force of 600 cavalry had gathered – armoured and well horsed – providing a formidable and mobile striking force to use against the insurgents.

A memorandum which has survived, records that decisions were also taken at Devizes to conscript 500 carpenters and 1000 or 2000 labourers, with quotas from counties all over England. Evidently the administrative process had been started from which the new castle projects of Conwy, Caernarvon and Harlech were to grow. These contingents were to meet at Chester on Sunday the 31st of May. As the king himself progressed northwards, little groups of men from the farthest parts of the kingdom were sharpening their tools and beginning to converge on Chester. A group of seventy men who left Newport Pagnell with a handcart for their tools, travelled there on foot.

Edward himself reached **Worcester** on the 16th of May and stayed there for seven days, issuing the summonses calling out the whole feudal host and appointing a rendezvous at Rhuddlan on August the 2nd. He moved to **Hartlebury** in Worcestershire on May the 23rd. The castle here had been built by Bishop Giffard, who in 1268 had obtained a royal license to complete its fortification. The king now called upon Giffard to furnish him with the fifty-six knights he owed him, by far the largest force of any of the king's tenants in Worcestershire. While at Hartlebury the king also made certain that orders were sent forbidding the movement out of the country of money recently collected by the clergy of the realm, to be used for a crusade to the Holy Land.

Edward's next stop was **Acton Burnell** in the marcher lands of Shropshire. This was a manor held since 1269 by Robert Burnell, Bishop of Bath and Wells, a firm friend and loyal servant of the king who was responsible for the intricate legislative programme of the reign. He was actively involved in the Welsh wars and evidently considered that his personal interests needed protecting in this exposed area of Shropshire. Between 1283–6 he built a fine fortified manor house there, most of which can still be seen.

The king spent only three days at Acton Burnell before moving to **Shrewsbury**, where doubtless he stayed in the castle. Thirteenth century work on the inner bailey with two circular towers is still preserved. The fine Welsh bridge with a fortified gateway, however, was unfortunately removed in the nineteenth century. From Shrewsbury three days march – via High Ercall and Adderley in Shropshire and Nantwich in Cheshire – brought the king and his gathering forces to Chester in the second week of June.

Chester was an advanced base of the English, strategically sited for striking into the mountainous heartland of the Welsh. A legionary fortress had been established here by the Romans, and Chester was linked to the capital via Watling Street (the A5). Troops could quickly reach the coast along the Dee estuary and patrol the Irish Sea. Here Edward stayed for the next twenty-seven days mustering his forces and planning the final subjugation of Wales by the acceleration of his castle-building programme.

The troops which gathered at Chester were accommodated in the countryside round the town, partly at Shotwick on the Dee, partly at Newton and Shocklach further inland. The cavalry were organised in three squadrons of one hundred lances each. There were problems with collecting enough "great horses at arms", for the king of France was refusing to allow the export of remounts: so Edward proclaimed that any person possessing thirty pounds yearly should provide himself "with a strong and suitable horse with befitting arms which may serve him in emergencies as often as shall be necessary". The foot on June the 15th numbered 7000. They came from all over the country and a large proportion were armed with bows; they are described as "*sagitarii*" (archers) rather than *pedites* (foot-soldiers). Enormous quantities of crossbow ammunition were stockpiled. 10,000 bolts or "quarrels" were sent from Bristol and another 14,000 soon after. To provide the labour force necessary for castle-building, bodies of carpenters and diggers converged on Chester. By the end of May 345 carpenters and 1000 diggers had arrived. The services of woodcutters were also required and William le Botiler of Wem in Shropshire got on with clearing the trees from the passes of "La Red Broc", "Batebriggemore" and "Cleley".

When the king decided to move westwards he adopted tactics similar to those employed in the first Welsh war of 1277. His forces were split into three armies, the two in the north planned to effect a pincer movement aimed at blockading Llywelyn in his stronghold of Snowdonia, while the army based on Carmarthen was supposed to attack Cardigan and force its way east towards Builth. The king himself advanced along the coast road towards Flint and Rhuddlan. His left flank was covered by Reginald de Grey, who took Hope Castle (nine miles south-west of Chester) from Dafydd's forces on June the 16th. He reached **Flint** on July the 7th.

The castle here had been under construction since 1277 when 2,300 labourers were engaged in digging the water defences. It was sufficiently far advanced to hold out successfully against Dafydd's surprise attack in March 1282. Its design was remarkable, being entirely surrounded by water fed from the estuary of the river Dee, so that it was fully accessible by ship. A square enclosure has a circular tower at three of its corners; the fourth being protected by a larger detached round-tower "keep" with a basement for the storage of clothing, ammunition, arms and armour, while the upper floors provided accommodation for the constable. An outer ward lay to the south, separated from the town by a moat.

The town itself was laid out along a series of parallel streets and was fortified. Edward had become acquainted with the idea of fortified towns (or "*bastides*") in his dominions of Gascony in south-west France. His idea was to attract English merchants and traders to settle, protected behind their walls, by offering them grants of land. The order went out to William de Perton, Constable at Flint, to deliver "to all wishing to have burgages or lands at Flynt, one burgage and forty acres of land and an acre of alderholt (woodland) to make a meadow there, quit of rent for ten years: after which time they shall render yearly 6d for the burgage and 3d for every acre of land or meadow".

Only five days later, on July the 12th, Edward arrived at **Rhuddlan**, where he was joined by the fleet, which which was now able to approach closely along the river Clwyd. This had involved the excavation of a new channel to replace the old meandering river bed, a formidable work of civil engineer-

CHESTER Cheshire
SJ 405665 OS 117
On the A56, twenty-five miles south of Liverpool. Roman legionary fortress with walls, remains of amphitheatre, and large collection of Roman remains in Grosvenor Museum. The walled city was extended in the middle ages, towers added, castle and Rows built. These last are streets with galleried arcades on top and in front of Roman buildings. A number of fine half timbered houses. St Werburgh's Abbey became cathedral in 1541 – mostly of the fourteenth century. See Guildhall Museum, Castle, Cheshire Regiment Museum, City Walls, and King Charles Tower Museum.

FLINT Flintshire
SJ 247734 OS 117
On the A548, ten miles north-west of Chester. A castle from which the coastal road from Chester to North Wales and passage to Ireland could be maintained, since it is on the Dee estuary, where the presence of firm rock decided the site. Rectangular "Bastide" town with a section for new town church and another for market – now partially obscured by railway, station, and Holyhead road.

RHUDDLAN Flintshire
SD 025778 OS 116
On the A547 three miles south of Rhyl. Rhuddlan was the site of two castles. The first, a Norman motte and bailey, is to the south on Twt Hill. Edward I's castle and town were founded together. There is a thirteenth century parish church with inscribed slabs from the Dominican Priory.

ing involving three years and an expenditure of £800 to complete. The castle itself had been designed by the Master Mason James of St George, whose daily wage at this time was two shillings. Master James was already experienced in building castles in Savoy in northern Italy, and there are many parallels between these and the Edwardian castles in Wales, which closely resemble them in style and design. The positioning of latrine shafts at Rhuddlan, and the diagonal inner angle of its corner towers are recognisable Savoyard techniques.

It is in the planning, however, that the mark of an architect of genius can be discerned. The castle is concentric, having two parallel lines of defence, one within the other. The outer ward, with its lower wall punctuated by towers, was surrounded by a dry moat except on the southern side, which was a fortified dock for shipping. The defence of the diamond shaped inner ward was a circuit of higher curtain walls, whose defenders could thus fire on an enemy assaulting the outer fortifications. The two entrances of the inner ward faced one another diagonally, and each was protected by an immensely strong gatehouse, flanked by a pair of circular towers. The town itself was another example of a "bastide", with an enclosing bank and ditch on three sides crowned by a wooden palisade: on the fourth side adequate defence was afforded by the steep river bank. The timber came from the forest of Delamere in Cheshire, and was later used for the new works at Caernarvon. "We command you to furnish our beloved sergeant at arms Thomas Carter with whatever he needs for the carriage of the Peel (palisade) and timber which were provided for enclosing the town of Rhuddlan, so that he can carry them to Caernarvon". The streets of the new town at Rhuddlan were laid out in the characteristic grid, and a bridge which completed the site was barricaded at night "For seven empty casks for making paling for the bridge at Rhuddlan 3s 8d. For locks bought to fasten the bars of the town and bridge by night 1s 6d."

During these two months journeying, it is likely that the king slept for the most part in castles and manor houses. When he arrived at Rhuddlan he evidently found the accommodation unfinished, since the timber buildings to lodge the king and the queen were still under construction in 1283. "To the same for eight thousand nails bought by him and for divers carriages of timber and boards bought for the Queen's chamber and for several houses of the castle and to the king's hall £2 17s 8d . . . To the carriage of turves to cover the king's kitchen 7s 6d . . . To six men carrying shingles to cover the hall of the castle, each receiving two and a half pennies per day for their wages for seven days. 8s 9d . . . for lime brought for the Queen's chamber in the castle 1s 8d . . . to Stephen the painter, painting the King's chamber and for colours bought by him and for his pay . . . 14s 0d". It is evident that the royal family meant to be here to stay. Even the queen's stew pond – where fish for the table were kept – was dug, fenced, a seat provided, water brought in, and the completed pond stocked with fish.

These sound like permanent quarters; but when he proposed to go campaigning in the depth of the winter of 1282, Edward assembled his camping equipment. On December the 21st he sent John de Dorset to his clerks William de Perton and Richard de Abingdon, ordering them to send his tents and pavilions. "They were also to send timber of ash and

A stretch of Conwy town wall, with the remains of two of its half-round lookout towers. Like Rhuddlan, the fortifications are the inspiration of prolific Master Mason James of St George

The River Conwy formed an important part of the town's natural defenses

carpenters to make stakes (presumably tent poles) therewith for the afore-said pavilions . . . so that of the aforesaid stakes 200 shall be shod with iron (*ferrale*) for the chamber and chapel of the king."

This rightly emphasises the fact that the organisation of the whole court was adapted for travelling. We know that when Edward was on his last campaign to Scotland in 1306–7, the royal party numbered 200. Apart from the members of the royal family, this number comprised the various officers of the household, including the keeper of the Wardrobe; the king's chaplain; two surgeons; two messengers; two porters and two trumpeters; seven valets of the king's chamber; and three *garciones* (boy servants or grooms). There were also twenty-three sumpters, whose job was the packing and transporting of household materials; two servants responsible for look-ing after the books, vestments and ornaments of the chapel; four servants of the wardrobe; fifty-five other servants connected with the kitchen, buttery, almonry and other departments; forty-five sumpters to transport the robes and bed of the king; and twenty-two grooms and huntsmen. To keep this great train in motion required strings of horses.

The horse, indeed, was essential to thirteenth century society in peace and war. The feudal cavalry which Edward I summoned to the Welsh or French wars was mounted on heavy "great" horses or "*destriers*": these were furnished with special saddles and stirrups enabling their riders to withstand the violence of mounted shock combat. The so-called "rounceys" and "hackneys", used as pack and draught animals, cost only ten pounds each compared with the great horses, which were valued in excess of fifty pounds apiece. There were also riding horses called "palfreys" and "cour-sers". All these horses ate large quantities of grain, a fact which led to a reluctance to replace the more economical but slower oxen as draught animals. They also required numerous grooms and stable boys under the supervision of the marshals of the stable and the clerk of the marshalsea: who accompanied the horses and supplied horseshoes, bridles, hobbles, ropes and other pieces of harness. Purchases of hay, oats, litter and brush-wood had to be made at various places along the itinerary, and stabling arranged. We are told that thirteen mowers, 160 spreaders of hay and six carts (each with three horses) were needed to bring in the hay harvest at Rhuddlan in 1283.

The provisioning of such a considerable body of people was a terrifying prospect for the host abbot or manorial lord, and the retinue of the court spread through the land like a herd of locusts. Lanercost Priory, indeed, never recovered from the experience of Edward I's last visit of 1306–7, and went into permanent decline in the later middle ages. The scale of supplies consumed by this peripatetic host while it was stationed at Rhuddlan can be calculated from such items in the accounts as these "To master William, the king's baker, for five carts hired by him, to carry meal from Chester to Rhuddlan 5s 10d . . . for the carriage of four casks filled with beans expended in the household, from the water (i.e. the dock at Rhuddlan) to the castle 2s 0d . . . Tuesday next before the feast of the Ascension of our Lord, paid for the carriage of thirty-four casks of wine from the water to the castle . . . for the carriage of wheat, viz. for 145 quarters from Good Friday to the Vigil of the Ascension of Our Lord from the water to the castle £1 3s 1d". When the queen arrived more trouble was taken to vary the royal diet. John of the Queen's Salsary (larder) was despatched to fish in the ponds of Stafford and to bring the fish to Rhuddlan. Richard the Forester was sent rabbiting, venison was brought down river from Chester, and cheese, honey and (a touch of the exotic) figs and raisins, were purchased.

The war in the meantime had not been going too well. The army in the South under the Earl of Gloucester had suffered a severe reverse at the hands of the Welsh at Llandeilo in June. Edward had called up the nobility and gentry of Somerset and Devon to reinforce the southern army. Evidently, as the king mentioned in a harshly worded writ to the sheriff, this official had been conscripting "the old and weak to go in the king's service to Wales and has spared the strong and powerful of arms in consideration of gifts (*pro muneribus*)". A ferocious threat followed: "if he be negligent or remiss, the king will so punish him that he shall feel himself aggrieved all his life". Fresh operations mounted by the new commander, William de Valence, had more success; and the whole of central Wales was in English hands by October. Llywelyn was forced to flee north to aid Dafydd.

In the meantime, the two armies in the north were again on the move. The fleet had assembled at Rhuddlan; on July the 10th the advanced squadron of twenty eight ships had began its fifteen days *servitium debitum* (unpaid feudal service). Several days later twelve more ships joined, and two great galleys. This whole force was put together from the Cinque Ports of Romney, Winchelsea, Hastings, Dover, Hythe and Sandwich. The strategy of the attack was the occupation of Anglesey, to be followed by the isolation and starvation of the Welsh in Snowdonia. The importance of Anglesey had been described by Giraldus Cambrensis thus; "when crops have failed in all other regions, this island from the richness of its soil and its abundant produce has been able to supply all Wales." Edward proposed to occupy the island and construct a bridge of boats over the Menai to Bangor. In August there were signs of great activity at Rhuddlan: timber, iron, nails, boats, anchors, cords and material of all kinds were being brought together. The king was told by the leaders of the Cinque Ports that he would need to make the boats for the bridge at Chester rather than try to send them round by sea from Kent. This advice was taken, and carpenters summoned from the Ports began making the pontoon-boats with a minimum of delay. A gang of sixty-three carpenters, whose wages were 3d a day, three foremen at 6d, and a master carpenter at 1s, were at work. The bridge was completed in September and the advance was resumed.

Edward's division overran the high land which composed the watershed between the Clwyd and the Conwy during October. His headquarters were at Llangernyw, near Llanwrst. Another thrust led to the capture of the castles at Denbigh and Dinas Bran. And though the English suffered a serious reverse when the Welsh routed the force trying to cross to Anglesey, the back of the rebel's resistance was soon afterwards broken by the unlooked for death of Llywelyn – killed almost casually in an ambush near Builth. In January 1283, then, Edward once again crossed the watershed of the Clwyd to the upper waters of the Conwy. He secured a base at Bettws y Coed and laid siege to nearby Dolwyddelan Castle. This sacred spot, the

CONWY Carnarvonshire
SH 784775 OS 115

Conwy is on the A55 four miles south of Llandudno. It is justly famous for its town walls, 1400 metres in length with three double gateways and twenty-one towers, which make it among the finest fortified towns in Europe. The castle is built in one corner. The parish church was built on the former site of the monastery of Aberconwy and incorporates some of it. Telford's road bridge of 1826 was built in mock thirteenth century style, and the railway is carried across the river by his Tubular Bridge. Both have been supplemented by a new bridge. There is a medieval house (Aberconwy) at the junction of Castle St. and High St. Also Plas Mawr, a fine Elizabethan House.

birthplace of Llywelyn the Great, was soon captured and the king then pushed on to **Conwy** and occupied the peninsula where he immediately began building the celebrated castle. This was to be his headquarters for the rest of the war.

The site of Conwy Castle has great natural defensive advantages; it is washed on three sides by the waters of the Conwy river and its tributary the Gyffin. It was also near a ready supply of building stone and was accessible by ship. From it the English could bottle up the Welsh in Snowdonia. They could also control the route along the north Wales coast. On the site of the future town there had stood a former residence of Llywelyn ap Gruffydd and also the buildings of the Cistercian abbey of Aberconwy, the spiritual centre of Gwynedd and the burial-place of Llywelyn the Great.

David, the last hope of the continuing Welsh resistance was now hemmed up in the wild region of Cader Idris in Merioneth. He was taken "by men of his own tongue" and handed over to the English in June 1283. The fearful penalties awaiting a medieval traitor were ordered to be carried out by the parliament meeting at Shrewsbury in October. David was hanged, drawn and quartered, his head being exposed on a pike at the Tower of London side by side with Llywelyn's. Edward I also settled the political problems of Wales in the next year by his statesmanlike statute of Rhuddlan. Castles continued to be built ensuring that the conquest would be permanent. Towns were founded ensuring the economic domination of the English. The county administration which prevailed in the county of Chester was extended over the newly conquered area. Wales in fact was now incorporated within the realm of England. Seldom has a single royal journey been attended by such momentous consequences.

Twin towers of Telford's suspension bridge reverently echo the shapes of Mason James' east Barbican

Eleanor of Castile
The Queen's last progress
HARBY–WESTMINSTER 1290

John Steane

Eleanor of Castile was the daughter of a famous father, Fernando III of Castile and Leon (d. 1252), whose conquest of Cordoba, Murcia and Seville from the Moors procured his canonisation. As part of an alliance between her half-brother Alfonso of Castile and Henry III, Eleanor married Henry's son Edward at Burgos in 1254. She was an affectionate wife: when Edward was being treated in Palestine in 1272 for a wound inflicted by a member of the sect of the Assassins, she was so noisily distraught that the physician ordered her from the room. Her graciousness eventually made her popular in England, despite being a foreigner. She could be an exacting landlord. She had an expensive taste for southern luxuries, importing exotic furnishings like Moorish majolica and Venetian glass. She loved Mediterranean fruit and keenly oversaw her garden at Langley (Hertfordshire), bringing back Spanish gardeners to improve it on her return from France in 1289. The next year she died. Her bowels were buried in Lincoln Cathedral and her heart was enshrined in a London friary. The rest of her body remains in the tomb in Westminster Abbey, on which is her gilt brass effigy, a marvellous evocation of feminine grace and piety.

On the 28th of November 1290, at Harby in Nottinghamshire, there occurred the death of Queen Eleanor of Castile, first wife of Edward I. This event had a remarkable architectural sequel, of interest to all would-be travellers of medieval England. Along the route followed by the corpse of his beloved queen, from Lincoln to its burial place in London, the king caused to be raised a series of twelve stone crosses, three of which can still be seen. Tombs of great splendour were also erected at Lincoln and in two places in London. This all amounted to "a monumental display more elaborate than that accorded to any English king or queen before or since" (Colvin).

Little is known in detail about the much romanticised figure of Queen Eleanor of Castile. Even her birth date is uncertain, but she was probably born in about 1240, the only daughter among five children born to Fernando III (c. 1200–1252), king of Castile and Leon in Spain, by his second wife, Jeanne of Dammartin. In pursuance of dynastic ambition, Henry III of England negotiated the marriage of his eldest son Edward with the Spanish princess; and they were united at the Cistercian convent of Las Huelgas near Burgos. Eleanor travelled to England in 1255. Henceforward her life was a strenuous and hectic mixture of travelling and child bearing. Her health was apparently robust, at any rate to begin with: she survived sixteen confinements and was not troubled by any of the congenital cardiac difficulties which plagued other members of the Castilian royal house. By 1290, however, only six of her children were still living, Eleanor (b. 1269), Joanna (b. 1272), Margaret (b. 1275), Mary (b. 1279), Elizabeth (b. 1282), and Edward of Caernarvon (b. 1284), due to become the future ill-fated Edward II.

Both Edward I and his queen spent much of their time travelling over their extensive dominions from the Cheviots to the Pyrenees. Such royal peregrinations fulfilled important political functions. During an age in which communications were only as speedy as a man on horseback and which knew no press photographers, a royal progress was the only way for the king and queen to be seen by most of their subjects. The fact that the king was liable to turn up in person made potential rebels think twice. Moreover accessibility was one of the keynotes of medieval monarchy. It appears that Eleanor of Castile was accustomed to receive her husband's subjects. There is an oft recounted tale that during one such progress at St Albans, the queen stopped her coach to hear the complaints of the townswomen against the abbot's exactions, and upbraided the abbot for trying to keep them away from her. The book of accounts of the last year of her life records that women brought to the queen humble gifts of fruit and a large loaf (*unum magnum panem*); evidently the common people regarded her as an easily approachable figure who might intervene on their behalf with her lord. Another appealing characteristic of Eleanor was the frequency with which she gave alms. In the last year of her life, between the 25th of April 1289 and the 28th of November 1290, she provided meals for no less than 9306 paupers at the cost of $1\frac{1}{2}$d per meal. In combination with the number fed by the king she must have contributed in no small way to the relief of the poor of the kingdom.

We can picture the peripatetic court (or *familia* as it was called) of the queen as it rumbled and creaked along the country lanes of thirteenth century England. The queen herself was surrounded by knights, ladies, damsels and various functionaries. At the head of the *familia* were administrators; these included the treasurer-keeper, John de Berewyk, the controller, Richard de Bures, and various "wardrobe" clerks responsible for her clothing, valuables and finance. There were twelve knights attached to the queen's household, and also a number of ladies, Margerie de Haustede, Ermentrude de Sackville, Juliana de Stourton, Alice le Breton. They each had their own tasks; Margerie, for example, was usually entrusted with keeping the queen's jewels. A number of damsels of noble family were also kept so that they might acquire the manners of courtly life. The ladies all travelled in a coach (*currus*), kept at the queen's expense. The queen was also surrounded by a crowd of servants known as *servientes, scutiferi, valletti* and *sumetarii* – "servants", "squires", "grooms" and "sumpters" or "packmen". These staffed the various offices into which the movable court was divided: the kitchen ("*coquina*"); the pantry and butlery "*panetaria butelaria*" (responsible for food and drink supplies); the wardrobe "*garderoba robarum*" (clothes and valuables); the chamber "*camera*" (responsible for the queen's private rooms) and the treasury. There were also several sub offices including the saucery ("*salsaria*") attached to the kitchen, the napery "*napparia*" (for plate and table linen) and the hall ("*aula*"). A major problem with multiple moves was packing up. The sumpters or porters were responsible for packing and carrying the coffers and chests containing the utensils. Each office had its own sumpter, a man experienced in handling the same objects time and time again. At times there were accidents. A cart turned over into the water when the court was passing through Burgh in September 1289 and some of the queen's clothes had to be repaired. The chief problem was the replacement of wheels and axles, and the road system of medieval England was littered with worn out pieces of the royal carts. Travel could also lead to injury. In 1287 an outrider of one of the wardrobe carts was so badly maimed in an accident with his cart that he could no longer carry on with his duties, and the king sent him to a religious house to be looked after.

How did the royal family recruit staff for their mobile households? Royal service in fact had a number of attractions. Wages were steady, food and clothing were provided for old age. Often the members of the household were interlinked by kinship, and the various family groups, (the Ferrers, Haustedes, Popcots and Stourtons) who served the crown in this way are found to be attaining baronial rank in the fourteenth century. In old age there might be corrodies (a form of insurance whereby the beneficiary was lodged free of cost in a monastery) and exchequer allowances. A typical instance of the care taken of old royal servants was the queen's coachman, Christian Page. From 1286 he began to lose his sight, and Michael "of the queen's coach" was brought up to assist. By 1290 Christian's sight was gone, and when he was sent back to Ponthieu in France, Michael was now ready to replace him. The *Liber* (account book) which records the accounts of Eleanor's court during the last year of her life occasionally provides details which flesh out our knowledge of the activities of this rather shadowy queen. We know, for instance, that she had a taste for rare and exotic objects from foreign countries. When she had arrived in England forty years before people had marvelled at the luxuriance of the Spanish cloths which were hung on the walls of the queen's apartments. In 1289–90 two pictured cloths were brought to the queen from Cologne by a German courtier. She bought basins of Damascene work, cloths from Tripoli and Venetian vases. Her delight in personal possessions is illustrated by the purchase of enamel caskets from Limoges and jewels from Parisian and Florentine merchants. All this added a note of brilliance to what was already the most efficient court in medieval Europe.

Eleanor's love of hunting is implied by payments to her falconer or *auceps*. We know from the king's wardrobe accounts that there were no less than thirty falconers engaged in training or maintaining the royal hunting birds. Young birds obtained by purchase or by gift from continental rulers were cared for in the mews at Charing Cross. Doves serving as food for falcons were kept in cotes; when on the move horses were furnished to carry cages for the birds. Medicinal supplies were also obtained, and when a bird was taken ill the falconer purchased wax to make a likeness of the ailing gerfalcon, to be placed at a shrine of St Thomas at Canterbury in the hope of a miraculous cure.

As she approached the end of her life it is likely that the queen's recreation was spent in quieter pursuits. Various sums of money were disbursed to minstrels who amused her; she also had two fools, Robert and Thomas. It is probable that she could read and write, comparatively rare accomplishments for the largely illiterate early medieval monarchy. Certainly there are plenty of references to the queen's scribes, Roger and Philip, and their associate, the *pictor* (painter or illuminator) Godfrey. Purchases of gold, vermilion, mucilage or "white gum of Spain" (*gumma alba de Ispannia*) ink and vellum are for the books of the queen. A coffer was provided "for the queen's romances" (*pro romanciis regine*) – so she was apparently an enthusiastic reader of the lesser productions of the French Arthurian cycle. Her interest in religion, implied by the psalter and prayer books bought at Cambridge, was perhaps more formal, but the numerous benefactions recorded in the *Liber* shows that she was a devoted patron to the Dominican Friars. She provided money for their food and drink at the provincial chapters of 1289 and 1290.

It seems that Queen Eleanor's health began to fail in the last four years of her life. The records provide an interesting commentary on the desperate measures – medical, magical, and religious – which were taken in an attempt to recover the queen's health. In the winter of 1285–6 medicines were provided and in the spring recourse was had to the old custom of *mensura* – or "measuring". This involved a wax candle of the patient's own height being sent to be burnt before the shrine of her favourite saint. Intercession would be begged for a return to health, or prayers offered to give thanks for her recovery. She was well enough to accompany her husband on his three year visit to France and Gascony but was described as suffering from a "quartan fever", which sounds like malaria, in 1287. This lingering malarial condition contributed to her death in 1290. The royal couple returned to England in August 1289 and in February 1290 a court goldsmith, William de Farendon, was paid £6 8s 4d, for making "images in the queen's likeness when she fell sick". In the same month she gave £100 to have a chapel prepared for the burial of her heart at the Dominican Priory of London, the same place where that of her son Alphonse had been buried. Both suggest that she had forebodings of her own death.

One would have thought, therefore, that she would have taken life a little more quietly, but there is no indication that she relaxed her furious spate of travelling during these last few months. She was with the king almost continually throughout the year, and accompanied him through Northamptonshire into Nottinghamshire in the late summer for the parliament to be held in the royal house at Clipstone from the 27th of October until the 11th of November. Once the business had been finished the king and queen began a progress from Clipstone to Lincoln. The journey was accomplished in a number of stages despite being only fifteen miles in length. They left Clipstone on the 13th of November and rested for a few days at the seat of Sir Adam de Eveningham at Laxton; then, on the 17th of November they proceeded to Marnham and Chaworth where two days were spent. On the 20th they arrived at **Harby**, a tiny village in Nottinghamshire, and here in the house of Sir Richard de Weston, the queen took to her sickbed.

In the meantime further medical help had been summoned. We hear of a physician, Master Peter of Portugal, especially sent for by the queen on the 23rd of September 1290. Syrups and other *medecinalia* (medicines) were bought at a cost of 13s 4d at Lincoln. Messengers were again sent to Lincoln with instructions to purchase urinals because of the queen's illness. It seems she was suffering from a low fever: the chronicler Wikes describes her as "modicae febris igniculo contubescens" – "swollen with a burning low fever". On the day of her death John Pederton was dispatched to Lincoln to buy *specia* (drugs), but she died after six in the evening on the 28th of November 1290.

The body was immediately removed to **Lincoln** and is traditionally said to have been embalmed in the Gilbertine priory of St Katherine in the southern suburb of the city. Evisceration – the removal of the bowels and other organs – preceded embalming. There is a curious entry in the *Liber* which clearly refers to the process: a bushel of barley (*pro uno bussello ardei*) was placed in the queen's body, and a pound of incense and six ells of cloth were provided. The queen's viscera were buried in the chapel of the Blessed Virgin Mary in Lincoln Cathedral. Edward and Eleanor had been present ten years before when the ceremonial translation of the body of St Hugh had taken place in the Cathedral, and it was fitting that a portion of the body of the queen should find its resting place in the Angel Choir. The heart was reserved for the church of the Dominican Friars in London. During his stay at Lincoln the king was lodged at Nettleham, three miles from the city. For five days the process of government ceased: evidently the king was in deep mourning, and no writs were issued until the second and third of December.

The funeral procession set out from Lincoln on the morning of the fourth of December. The first stage taken by the sad cortège is uncertain. A progress by the Fosse Way to Newark was argued by Stevenson, but a more direct route was to follow Ermine Street and strike due south to **Grantham**,

HARBY Nottinghamshire
SK 878705 OS 121
Harby is three miles south of the A57 between Lincoln and Worksop six miles west of Lincoln. All Saints church has a sculpture of Eleanor of Castile in the east wall of the tower and a brass plate recording her death inside. The site of the manor of Richard de Weston is to the east of the church. This is where Eleanor died.

LINCOLN Lincolnshire
SK 978718 OS 121
Lincoln is on the A46 seventeen miles north-east of Newark-on-Trent. Lincoln stands where the Jurassic ridge (a belt of limestone) is cut by the river Witham. Originally a Roman legionary fortress with a colonia extending down Steep Hill to the river. Parts of the Roman defences are visible (East Gate, Lower West Gate). It was later a Danish town (finds in museum) and an important medieval city with castle and cathedral sited spectacularly on top of the ridge. Most of the cathedral had been built by Eleanor's time. The core of the west front is Norman, the rest is c.1190–1280, including the magnificent Angel choir, but the towers were added in the fourteenth century. There are two medieval stone houses (Aaron the Jews house, the Jews house) and a medieval guild hall across the river. The castle has Norman work and a terrifying gaol. The City and Country Museum is in a Franciscan church and the Museum of Lincolnshire Life is in an old barracks on Burton Road.

GRANTHAM Lincolnshire
SK 913363 OS 130
On the A607 twenty-five miles south of Lincoln. An important medieval market town with thirteenth century church of St Wulfram, which has a massive tower and soaring spire, 272 ft high. Grantham House is fourteenth century and there is a fifteenth century Grammar School (where Isaac Newton was a pupil). The Angel and Royal Inn is also medieval.

117

The site of Richard de Weston's manor at Harby is revealed by this gently undulating land behind the church

An aspect of the south side of Lincoln's magnificent cathedral

Gated entrance to Bulwick Park

The Queen Eleanor Cross at Geddington

Geddington's fine thirteenth century bridge

The gleamingly clean, but sadly now incomplete Cross at Hardingstone

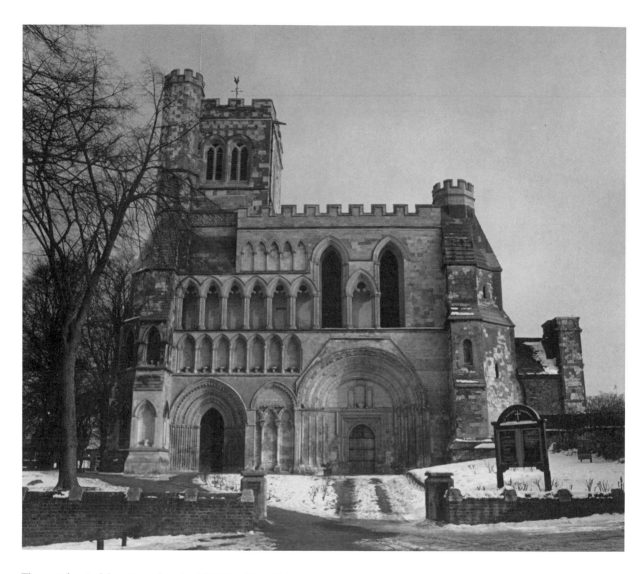

The west front of the priory church of St Peter, Dunstable

where afterwards one of the Eleanor crosses was raised. It is certain that the procession stopped at **Great Casterton** – north of Stamford – on the fifth, because documents are attested there. The usual route to London from Stamford was via Wansford to Huntingdon and thence by Royston, Puckeridge and Cheshunt. In fact a more westerly route was chosen through more frequented parts where the queen was well known. It was also a part of the plan to take in some of the religious houses on the way. The next twenty miles or so south has some interesting relics of medieval roads. The medieval and modern routes from Stamford to **Easton-on-the-hill** coincide in the A43. At Easton-on-the-Hill the present road follows the line of a turnpike built in the eighteenth century to avoid a double bend in the main street, while a modern by-pass short circuits the twisting and narrow medieval street of the village of **Duddington** along which the funeral procession passed. The medieval road can be seen as a hollow way preserved in **Bulwick Park** about 200 metres to the north west of the present A43. At Deenethorpe also the medieval route has now been byepassed; but the ancient road can be seen in another hollow way to the south of the village. The patches of woodland remind us that this was the ancient royal forest of Rockingham, favourite hunting country of the Angevin kings. At **Geddington** (where the medieval road takes a sharp right angled turn to the east) was a royal palace, sited to the north of the parish church. Here the body of the queen rested for a night. One of the three surviving Eleanor crosses was erected in the centre of the village. In the morning the procession moved over the thirteenth century bridge whose gothic arches and massive cutwaters still span the river Ise, and so on past the village of Kettering to **Northampton**. To the south of that town was the house of the Cluniac nuns of **Delapré**; here the body rested again, and on the old main road to London at **Hardingstone** another cross was erected which survives till today.

Shortly afterwards the procession struck Watling Street (one of the great roads of the kingdom since Roman times and now represented by the A5) and stopped at **Stony Stratford**. Thence it deviated in its route towards the capital by way of a succession of famous shrines. Stops were made at **Woburn Abbey** (a house of Cistercian monks) and at **Dunstable**. In the Annals of Dunstable we read that the body rested there one night and that the king made offerings of two rich cloths of "Baudekyn" and four score pounds of wax for candles. After spending the night in the priory church, "the bier rested in the market place until the king's chancellor and the great men there present had marked a fitting place where they might afterwards erect, at the king's expense, a cross of wonderful size". When the procession approached **St Albans** the whole convent, solemnly wearing their hoods, went out as far as the church of St Michael at the entrance of the town to meet it. The body was placed before the high altar of the abbey church (now the cathedral) and all night long the monks engaged in divine offices and holy vigils. At this point the king left the procession and preceded it to London. The last stopping place was **Waltham Abbey**, again a deviation from the direct route, doubtless taken because here was a royal monastery founded by King Harold – the home of a miraculous crucifix which gave the place its name of "Waltham Holy Cross" even before

GREAT CASTERTON Lincolnshire
SK 000092 OS 141
An attractive stone built village by the A1 two and half miles north-west of Stamford. Excavations have revealed a Roman town and villa – the earthworks are still visible, although now under the plough. The church dates from the Norman period and has thirteenth century additions.

EASTON-ON-THE-HILL
Northamptonshire
TF 013045 OS 141
On the A43 two miles south of Stamford. The priest's house at the west end of the village belongs to the National Trust and dates from the fifteenth century.

DUDDINGTON Northamptonshire
SK 989009 OS 141
On the A43 four miles south of Stamford. A small village in the stone belt with noteworthy seventeenth and eighteenth century houses (including a manor house dated 1633). Medieval church and fourteenth century bridge.

BULWICK PARK Northamptonshire
SP 963943 OS 141
On the A43 half-way between Stamford and Corby. Fine wrought iron gates into Bulwick Park, whose Hall dates from 1676. Two and a quarter miles NNE of Bulwick and visible from the main road are the earthworks of Hely, a castle deserted before the foundation of the Augustinian priory. This was destroyed in 1749 but the stables of the house succeeding it still stand.

GEDDINGTON Northamptonshire
SP 895831 OS 141
On the A43 four miles north of Kettering. On the edge of Boughton Park, home of Dukes of Buccleuch, who are commemorated in the chancel of Warkton church, two miles to the south. The village of Geddington has been by-passed to the west by the modern A43. The church includes Saxon work. The Palace site was to the north-east, but is now under a housing estate. The Eleanor cross is the best of the three surviving, and is in the centre of the village. The bridge is thirteenth century.

DELAPRÉ ABBEY Northamptonshire
SP 755590 OS 152
Half a mile south of Northampton, on the A508 which links with the M1, it stands in a park. Fragments of the Cluniac nunnery are incorporated in the seventeenth and eighteenth century house, now the home of the County Record Office and County Record Society.

HARDINGSTONE, QUEEN ELEANOR'S CROSS.

SP 755583 OS 152

On the London Road (A508) one mile south of Northampton. Begun in 1291 by John of Battle. Octagonal, with three tiers, it stands high on steps. Recently (1985) cleaned.

NORTHAMPTON

SP 755605 OS 152

On the A45 fourteen miles south-west of Kettering. A late Saxon town, where remains of Saxon palaces were found in 1983–4. Has a massive market square with All Saints church. The church of the Holy Sepulchre (Sheep Street) is a rare twelfth century round church. Insignificant fragments of the Norman castle, one of the most important royal stongholds in England, stand by the Castle railway station. Nearby is the fine Norman St Peter's church (Mare fair). The Central Museum, Guildhall, has archaeological collections. Abington Park Museum and Regimental Museum occupy a house lived in by Shakespeare's grand-daughter.

STONY STRATFORD,

Buckinghamshire
SP 787405 OS 152

On the A5 (Watling Street) with eighteenth century houses and Cock and Bull Inns. Best seen on a Sunday, when there is less traffic.

WOBURN ABBEY, Bedfordshire

SP 965327 OS 165

A Cistercian abbey founded in 1145. The cloister was probably situated under present stately home, where a courtyard between three wings now exists. The buildings of the abbey came into the possession of John Lord Russell, first Earl of Bedford. The house was rebuilt in the seventeenth and eighteenth centuries.

DUNSTABLE, Bedfordshire

TL 018218 OS 166

On the A5 five miles west of Luton. A Roman posting station at the junction of Watling Street and the Icknield Way. The Augustinian priory church of St Peter was founded by Henry I in 1131–2.

the third surviving memorial to Queen Eleanor was built there. As the body of the queen was approaching London, the king, accompanied by the nobility, prelates and other clergy, went out to meet it. It is not known where the body rested in London for the three days prior to the entombment on 17th December, but crosses were subsequently raised at the king's mews at **Charing**, and at **Westcheap**, which is near St Paul's Cathedral.

The funeral rites in Westminster Abbey were performed with great magnificence: "*cum summa omnium reverentia et honore*" ("with all possible reverence and honour") says Walsingham. But Edward I intended a more lasting memorial, and he entrusted the erection of tombs and crosses to the queen's three executors: Robert Burnell, Bishop of Bath and Chancellor; Henry de Lacy, Earl of Lincoln; and a clerk named John of Berwick, keeper of the wardrobe of the late queen. In turn they delegated the task to two clerks whose business it was to wind up the queen's estate, make various bequests named in her will, and erect the memorials.

The two principal tombs of Queen Eleanor were raised at Lincoln and Westminster. Master William Torel, a London goldsmith, received a total remuneration of £138 13s 4d for casting two bronze effigies by the *cire-perdue* ("lost-wax") process. The records, indeed, mention large quantities of wax (eg. *Item, in cariagio, DCC, XXVI lib cerae de domo magistri Willielmi Torel, usque domum Domini*, "Item, for carrying 726 pounds of wax from the house of Master William Torel to the Lord's house"). Metal was bought from William Sprot and John of Ware; and a quantity of gold florins were purchased from merchants of Lucca for the gilding. The effigies were cast in the yard of the abbey. They were technically remarkable as some of the first bronze effigies cast in England. And despite their thickness, which suggests that Torel had not completely mastered his medium, they are artistically assured; "the high forehead, shape of the crown, thick neck and firm chin, the slight sway of the figure" being notable. The effigy at Westminster lies on a tomb chest fashioned of marble by Richard of Crundale. It was protected by a wooden cover made by Thomas of Houghton and painted by Walter of Durham – who was later to construct the throne on which British monarchs are still crowned. An intricate grille, made of wrought iron by Thomas of Leighton (in Bedfordshire) still guards the tomb. The Lincoln effigy was cast in 1293 and set up on a tomb made by the sculptors, Alexander of Abingdon and Nicholas Dymenge. Unfortunately it was destroyed in 1641, but a drawing made by Sir William Dugdale shows it to have been virtually identical with the one at Westminster.

We have no drawing or description of the heart burial in the church of the Black or Dominican Friars, London, but it certainly incorporated three small metal images and was probably sited in a side chapel. We know much more about the construction of the twelve crosses, because detailed information about nine of them survives in the accounts of the queen's executors. Charing Cross had a large amount of Purbeck marble used in its construction, supplied by Ralph of Chichester, and this accounts for its heavy cost, at least £700. The mason was Richard of Crundale who had gained experience over several years at Westminster Abbey. Michael of Canterbury contracted to build the cross at West Cheap for £226 13s 4d. Two more court masons built Waltham Cross, Roger of Crundale and Nicholas

The great circular window in Waltham Abbey looks out onto the tomb of King Harold

The perhaps rather too sharply restored Queen Eleanor memorial in Waltham Cross, now finds itself in the centre of a frantic traffic junction

Dymenge, the Caen stone statues being provided by Alexander of Abingdon and the total recorded cost coming to over £110. Five of the more northerly crosses were entrusted to Master John of Battle who, with his associates, was responsible for those at Northampton, Stony Stratford, Woburn, Dunstable and St Albans. Each cost over £100. There is no surviving information about the construction of the three remaining crosses at Stamford, Grantham and Geddington but presumably they were built between 1295 and the financial crisis of 1297 which put a brake upon the other royal works.

The appearance of the crosses may be judged from the three survivors, at Waltham, Northampton (Hardingstone) and Geddington. Those at Waltham and Northampton are polygonal. The pedestals are decorated with shields of Ponthieu, Castile, Leon, and England (this feature is also mentioned as being included in the now vanished cross at Stamford, and is seen in the carved fragments of the Westcheap cross). At Northampton at this stage there are representations of books, open on a lectern, which were presumably originally covered with a painted inscription. The second stage of Waltham and Northampton is an octagon formed of a pillar. In front of each side is a statue of the queen under an elaborate gabled and vaulted canopy. Behind them and above rises the central shaft which would originally have terminated in a cross. At Geddington the same features are skilfully adapted to a triangular plan.

The final question to be considered are the motives behind this monumental display. Undoubtedly the crosses demonstrate Edward's reverence for the memory of his queen. Theirs is a virtually unique example of a happy and affectionate marriage in a world where dynastic marriages were arranged despite and not because of love between the partners. But this is not to deny that they also reflect Edward's determination to enhance the prestige of the English monarchy "by creating visible symbols of its piety and power" (Colvin). The fact that they were distributed along some of the main roads and near the shrines of the kingdom is an indication of forethought. Edward was, in fact, imitating the example of the French; similar memorials had been set up twenty years before to mark the route of the funeral procession of King Louis IX (later canonised as St Louis) from Paris to St Denis. While Edward's idea of creating a royal mausoleum in Westminster Abbey around St Edward the Confessor's shrine was also probably an attempt to emulate the idea of the same King Louis, who set up effigies of his ancestors in the church of St Denis.

ST ALBANS, Hertfordshire
TL 145071 OS 166
On the A5 twenty miles north-west of London. Important remains of Roman town at Verulamium, two miles to the south-east of the town (including theatre, hypocaust and fine museum). The cathedral was, during the middle ages, the abbey church of one of the greatest English Benedictine monasteries. It has a tremendous length of Norman nave, and tower and transepts built in re-used Roman brick. The fourteenth century monastic gateway is now a school. Medieval Fighting Cocks Inn, Saxon St Michael's Church and fifteenth century clock tower in the market place. There is also a City Museum, Gorhambury House and Kingsbury Watermill Museum.

WALTHAM CROSS, Essex
TL 362004 OS 166
Situated on the A10, the London/ Cambridge Road. Probably more complete than any of the other surviving crosses, but over restored. The Four Swans Inn dates from c.1260.

WALTHAM ABBEY, Essex
TL 381007 OS 166
Situated one and three quarter miles east of Waltham Cross. The abbey church was founded by King Harold, who was buried here after being slain at Hastings. Magnificent Norman nave, fifteenth century abbey gateway and medieval bridge.

CHARING CROSS, London
TQ 302806 OS 177
Outside and to the north of the present Charing Cross railway terminus. At the meeting of King Street, which connects with the Palace of Westminster, and Akeman Street (where Whitehall now enters Trafalgar Square) a cross was set up, the most expensive of the twelve (being of Caen stone and Purbeck marble) between 1291–4. The Roundheads pulled it down, and Royalists set up a statue of Charles I here after the Restoration. In front of Charing Cross station is what is claimed to be a replica of the old cross.

WESTCHEAP, 'Site of Cross' and 'London'
TQ 321813 OS 177
Cheapside takes its name from the Anglo-Saxon ceap (to sell or barter) and this was formerly the chief market of the city. In the middle of the street facing St Peter's church was the Eleanor Cross erected in 1290, renewed in the 1440s, frequently regilded at coronations and finally demolished in 1643. The church of St Mary le Bow has a Norman undercroft.

FURTHER READING

Boudicca

Dudley, D. R. and Webster, G., *The Rebellion of Boudicca*, London, 1962
Frere, S. S., *Britannia*, London, 1967
Rivet, A. L. F., *Town and Country in Roman Britain*, London, 1964

Alfred the Great

Asser, "Life of King Alfred" in Keynes, S. and Lapidge, M. (eds.), *Alfred the Great*, Harmondsworth, 1983
The Anglo-Saxon Chronicle (ed. G. N. Garmondsway), London, 1972
Hinton, D. A., *Alfred's Kingdom*, London, 1977

William the Conqueror

The Anglo-Saxon Chronicle; "Florence of Worcester"; William of Jumièges; and William of Poitiers, all in
    English Historical Documents 1042–1189 (Douglas, D. C. and Greenaway, G. W. (Eds.)) London, 1981
Darby, H. C. and Campbell, F, M. J. (Eds.), *The Domesday Geography of South-East England*, London,
    1962
Darby, H. C. and Versey, G. R., *Domesday Gazeteer*, London, 1977
Douglas, D. C., *William the Conqueror*, London, 1964

William Rufus

Barlow, F., *William Rufus*, London, 1983
Bloch, M., *Feudal Society*, London, 1961

King Stephen

Appleby, J. T., *The Troubled Reign of King Stephen*, London, 1969
Beeler, J., *Warfare in England 1066–1189*, Ithaca, New York, 1966
Cronne, H. A., *The Reign of Stephen*, London, 1970

King John

Fowler, G., "King John's Treasure", *Proceedings of the Cambridge Antiquarian Society* XLV, 1952
Hardy, T. D., "Itinerarium Johannis Regis Angliae". A Table of the movements of the court of King John
    from 1199 to the end of his reign. *Archaeologia* XXII, 1829
Holt, J. C., *Magna Carta*, Cambridge, 1965
Jenkinson, A. V., "The Jewels lost in the Wash", *History*, Oct. 1923
Norgate, K., *John Lackland*, London, 1902
Pafford, J. H. P., "King John's tomb in Worcester Cathedral", *Transactions of Worcestershire Archaeological
    Society*, N.S. XXXV, 1958
Pegge, S., "An enquiry into the nature and cause of King John's death", *Archaeologia* IV, 1777
Poole, A. L., *From Domesday Book to Magna Carta, 1087–1216*, Oxford, 1964
St. John Hope, W. H., "The loss of King John's Baggage Train in the Wellstream in Oct. 1216", *Archaeologia*
    LX, 1906

Edward I

Bund, J. W. Willis, *Episcopal Registers of Bishop Godfrey Giffard 1268–1301*, Worcestershire Historical
    Society 1902
Byerly, B. F. and Byerly, C. K., *Records of the Wardrobe and Household 1285–6*, H.M.S.O. London,
    1977
Calendar of Chancery Rolls (Various) 1277–1326, Public Records Office, London, 1912
Edwards, J. G. (Ed), *Calendar of Ancient Correspondence Concerning Wales*, Cardiff, 1935
Lysons, S., Copy of a roll of the expenses of King Edward I at Rhuddlan Castle in Wales, *Archaeologia*,
    XVI, 1812
Moorman, J. R. H., "Edward I at Lanercost Priory", *English Historical Review* CCLXII, April 1952
Morris, J. E., *The Welsh Wars of King Edward the First*, Oxford, 1901
Ralegh Radford, C. A., "The Medieval defences of Shrewsbury", *Shropshire Archaeological Society
    Transactions*, LVI 1957–60
Taylor, A. J., "Castle-building in Wales in the later thirteenth century: the prelude to construction" in Jope,
    E. M. (Ed) *Studies in Building History*, London, 1961
Gerald of Wales (ed. L. Thorpe), *The Journey through Wales and the Description of Wales*, Harmondsworth,
    1978

Eleanor of Castile

Brown, R. Allen; Colvin, H. M.; Taylor, A. J., *The History of the King's Works*, London, HMSO 1963
Botfield, B. & Turner, T., *Manners and Household Expenses of England in the 13th and 15th centuries*,
    Roxburgh Club, 1841
Byerly, B. F. and Byerly, C. K., *Records of the Wardrobe and Household, 1285–1286*, London, HMSO
    1977
Hartshorne, C. H., "Illustrations of domestic manners during the reign of Edward I", *Journal of the British
    Archaeological Association*, XVIII, 1862
Hunter, J., "On the death of Eleanor of Castile, Consort of King Edward the First, and honours paid
    to her memory", *Archaeologia*, XXIX, 1842
Liber quotidianus contrarotularis garderobae Anno regni regis Edwardi I vigesimo octavo 1299–1300,
    London, 1782
Parsons, J. C., *The Court and Household of Eleanor of Castile in 1290*, Toronto, 1977
Stevenson, W. H., "The Death of Queen Eleanor of Castile", *English Historical Review*, III.
Stevenson, W. H., "The Death of Queen Eleanor of Castile in Nottinghamshire", *Transactions of the
    Thoroton Society*, 1899, Supplement
Vetusta Monumenta quae ad Rerum Britannicarum memoriam conservandam, Society of Antiquaries,
    London, 1796